The First Amendment

Other titles in *The Constitution:*

The First Amendment
Freedom of Speech, Religion, and the Press
ISBN: 0-89490-897-9

The Second Amendment
The Right to Own Guns
ISBN:0-89490-925-8

The Fourth Amendment
Search and Seizure
ISBN: 0-89490-924-X

The Fifth Amendment
The Right to Remain Silent
ISBN: 0-89490-894-4

The Thirteenth Amendment
Ending Slavery
ISBN: 0-89490-923-1

The Fifteenth Amendment
African-American Men's Right to Vote
ISBN: 0-7660-1033-3

The Eighteenth and Twenty-First Amendments
Alcohol—Prohibition and Repeal
ISBN: 0-89490-926-6

The Nineteenth Amendment
Women's Right to Vote
ISBN: 0-89490-922-3

The First Amendment

Freedom of Speech, Religion, and the Press

Leah Farish

This is dedicated to my dear Brian and Colleen, who at times gave up some of their freedom of expression and association so that their mother could write this book.

With thanks to:
Bernard Schwartz, John Whitehead, Kelly Shackleford, and Richard D. White, Jr.

Library of Congress Cataloging-in-Publication Data

Farish, Leah.
The First Amendment: freedom of speech, religion, and the press/ Leah Farish.
p. cm. — (The constitution)
Includes bibliographical references and index.
Summary: Discusses the definition and history of the First Amendment and considers present day problems regarding the rights it guarantees.
ISBN 0-89490-897-9
1. Freedom of speech—United States—Juvenile literature. 2. Freedom of religion—United States—Juvenile literature. 3. Freedom of the press—United States—Juvenile literature. 4. Constitutional amendments—United States—1st—Juvenile literature. [1. Freedom of speech. 2. Freedom of religion. 3. Freedom of the press.] I. Title. II. Series: Constitution (Springfield, Union County, N.J.)
KF4770.Z9F37 1998
342.73'0853—dc21 97-13911
CIP
AC

Printed in the United States of America.

10 9 8 7 6 5 4 3 2

Photo Credits: AP Photo/Richard Sheinwald, p. 19; AP/Wide World Photos, pp. 40, 44; © Charles Wilson Peale, *James Madison*, 1792, oil on canvas, 0126.1006, From the Collection of Gilcrease Museum, Tulsa, p. 31; Congress of the United States, House of Representatives, p. 58; Copyright 1996, Austin American-Statesman, p. 62; Jennifer Warburg, p. 25; James Earl Frasier, *Thomas Jefferson*, bronze, 0817.168, From the Collection of Gilcrease Museum, Tulsa, p. 69; John Vanderlin, *Washington and Lafayette at the Battle of Brandywine*, oil on canvas, 0126.1018, From the Collection of Gilcrease Museum, Tulsa, p. 9; Leah Farish © 1996, pp. 13, 76; National Archives, p. 78; National Right to Life, p. 84; Richard Strauss, Collection of the Supreme Court of the United States, p. 71.

Cover Photo: AP/Wide World Photos.

Contents

1

Why Have a First Amendment?

Suppose for a moment that you are a student in a public school who has been named to give the graduation speech. You have worked long and hard on the speech. In it, you quote various historical figures from Plato to Dr. Martin Luther King, Jr. You check your speech with your principal as required. The principal says, "This is a wonderful speech. But we will have to cut the quote from Jesus—you cannot have any religious elements in your speech." What does the First Amendment say?

- Suppose that you log onto a computer network. You find that a group of people is discussing a certain ethnic group in a negative, vicious way. What does the First Amendment say?
- Imagine that you are a young, eager businessman hurrying to your monthly club meeting for lunch. You look forward to seeing lots of friends there and making useful connections with people who will help your business. When you walk in, you

find several people upset, while others are cracking jokes. It has been announced that your club has been ordered to allow new members: women. What does the First Amendment say?

- What if you get a summer job at an amusement park, and after a while you find out that the park owners are not obeying certain health and safety laws. You think about calling a newspaper to report the problems and picketing the place. What does the First Amendment say?

The First Amendment is only one sentence long, so the answers to these questions are very short. Yet they are also complex. Many laws are based on the First Amendment, and many thousands of legal cases have interpreted it. The First Amendment deserves a great deal of study. Debates on its meaning and application continue today.

Our Constitution and its first ten amendments were written by many of the same people who led the American Revolution—the war against England from 1775 until 1783. Our American revolutionaries distrusted human nature and believed that it had a natural tendency to grasp power.

Therefore, our Founding Fathers were not content to get rid of their British king and start in the United States with a new king. Instead, they wanted to build into their government some limits so that abuses of power could not happen.[1]

Early Americans built their new laws on a foundation of beliefs that rang loud and clear in the First Amendment. Understanding these beliefs helps us apply the First Amendment to our own lives.

This Painting by John Vanderlin shows George Washington (left) and Marquis de Lafayette during the Battle of Brandywine in the American Revolution. The United States Constitution and Bill of Rights were written by many of the leaders of the Revolutionary War.

1. First, there was a belief that a higher law existed over all, from which government borrowed any power and by which any government would be judged.
2. Second, the founders believed that all people deserved equal treatment. (Slavery, however, would not be uprooted from our economic base for seventy years, although many Founding Fathers opposed it from the start.)[2] These two beliefs led to the speech, press, and religion clauses in the First Amendment.[3]
3. Another belief was that local communities and groups had the right to form around certain ideas

AMERICAN	OTHER
Higher Law	
1. "[T]he smiles of heaven can never be expected on a nation that disregards the eternal rules of order and right which Heaven itself has ordained."[4] "If you ask an American who is his master, he'll tell you he has none. And he has no governor but Jesus Christ."[6]	**1.** "We say: morality is what serves [in] creating a new communist society. . . . We do not believe in eternal morality."[5] "The state, in fact, as the universal ethical will, is the creator of right."[7]
Equality	
2. "We hold these truths to be self-evident, that all men are created equal, that they are endowed by their creator with certain inalienable rights."	**2.** "The weak and the botched shall perish."[8] "Organization is putting the heads above the masses and subjecting the masses to the heads."[9]
Community Rule	
3. "[We] associate and conjoin ourselves to be as one public state or commonwealth; and . . . enter into combination and confederation together; to maintain and pursue the liberty and purity of the gospel of our Lord. . . ."[10] "[This state shall be] democraticall [sic], that is, a government held by the free and voluntary consent of all. . . ."[12]	**3.** "[R]esponsibility can and must be borne always by one man and thus he alone can have the authority and right of command."[11] "A few men, but great ones, will build a world wth their muscular arms on the corpses of the weak, the sick, the infirm."[13]
Written Law	
4. ". . . [W]hat any man undertakes to prove as necessary, he shall make good out of the Scriptures."[14] "The Framers of the Bill of Rights believed in . . . an immutable [unchangeable] Constitution."[16]	**4.** "All that can be expected . . . is that [our law] should easily and quickly . . . modify itself in accordance with the will of the . . . supreme power in the community. . . ."[15] "The will of a class is at times best expressed by a dictator."[17]

and ways of life. This led to the Freedom of Association Clause in the First Amendment.

4. Finally, the Founding Fathers believed that a written form of the law was better than having a king, dictator, or court tell them what the law was from day to day. The custom in church government was to argue a point "from authority" (for them, the Bible); and church custom, more than monarchy, was the model for the new American state. This led to the approach of letting the Supreme Court of the United States interpret the Constitution and federal laws. It confined the Court to only that role, however. In this book we will be looking at many Supreme Court decisions. Some of these examples will give us a sense of how the American view differs from those of other nations.

With these beliefs in mind, the framers of the Constitution created a foundation document for our nation. It has endured for over two hundred years. It grants certain powers from the people to the state governments and other powers to the federal, or national, government. It also separates federal powers into three branches: executive (President), legislative (Congress), and judicial (federal courts, the highest being the Supreme Court).

Once the Constitution was written, however, concerns continued that government could still grow too big and limit people's liberty. Patriots such as Patrick Henry insisted that a Bill of Rights be added to make clear the fact that rights such as free speech could not be limited by the government. Others, such as Alexander Hamilton, believed that a Bill of Rights would be "not only unnecessary in the proposed Constitution, but would even be dangerous."[18] They felt that to try to say all the things that government may not do would lead people to think government could do everything else that was not listed.

Many citizens sent to Congress ideas for the list of protected rights—211 in all![19] Congress discussed these and reduced the total number to twelve. Three fourths of the thirteen original states were needed to pass the twelve amendments that were being considered. After two years of debate, on December 15, 1791, Virginia became the tenth state to approve ten of the twelve. Those ten amendments became our Bill of Rights. One scholar says, "It would not be incorrect to call them a Bill of Prohibitions instead of a Bill of Rights, for . . . [they] are less a list of rights than they are a series of protections of rights."[20]

The First Amendment reads:

> Congress shall make no law respecting an establishment of religion, or prohibiting the free exercise thereof; or abridging the freedom of speech, or of the press, or the right of the people peaceably to assemble, and to petition the Government for a redress of grievances.

It is just one sentence, yet it affects many areas of our lives each day.

The three branches of federal government, as well as the state and local governments, are all continuously affected by the First Amendment. They may act to protect rights that the First Amendment protects; or they may act in ways that violate those rights. In that case, they would be called upon to change by some other branch of the government. Here are some examples:

- A city may write a local law against animal sacrifice. Those who believe in animal sacrifice might bring a lawsuit, because the law violates

David Blake, Dean of the Cox School of Business at Southern Methodist University, says, "There's never been anything like the Web. For business, it's as important as Gutenburg's discovery of the printing press. For society, it ranks up there with the movement of people from farms to villages." However, the use of the Internet raises some First Amendment questions.

their freedom of religion. The Supreme Court, or a lower court, might uphold the law or strike it down.[21]

- An agency under the control of the President of the United States might send out a letter to all local school districts, to tell them what religious activities should be allowed on public school campuses. A local school board might vote to implement some of the guidelines and reject others.[22]
- On the other hand, Congress could pass a law that calls for criminal penalties for the display of obscene images over computer networks. It would be up to the Supreme Court to apply the First Amendment to that law.[23]

A dramatic struggle between our branches of government has occurred over the last few years. A state commission ruled that two Native Americans could be fired from their jobs for smoking peyote. The United States Supreme court agreed. But then the United States Congress voted to void that decision with the Religious Freedom Restoration Act. It protects religious observances such as the ritual smoking of peyote. The act was in turn ruled an unconstitutional exercise of the power of Congress.[24] What will happen next is anyone's guess.

One of the fascinating effects of the First Amendment is that it balances one level, or branch, of our government against another; or, one good against another good. That longstanding, healthy tension in our society is a sign of the wisdom of those who set up our government as well as of those who participate in it today—and that includes all people in the United States.

2

Freedom of Speech

In a 1920 speech in Moscow, Russian communist leader Vladimir Ilyich Lenin said:

> Why should freedom of speech and freedom of the press be allowed? Why should a government which is doing what it believes to be right allow itself to be criticized? It would not allow opposition by lethal weapons. Ideas are much more fatal than guns. Why should any man be allowed to buy a printing press and [spread dangerous] opinions calculated to embarrass the government?[1]

It is true that free speech can be a dangerous thing. Americans, however, have decided that it is so important that we will not only allow it, but protect it.

The speech held so dear by the framers of the Constitution was basically limited to that produced by the scratch of the quill pen on parchment, the squeaky printing press, and the human voice. Over two centuries later we also value speech carried over telephones and modems, between satellites and cellular phones, on laser printers, on radios, and on movie screens.

We now recognize the freedom to express ourselves as groups, through art, and through our clothing and actions. We have also established the principle that the government cannot make us express something that we do not wish to say. The First Amendment has also been found to guarantee our right to receive other people's expression, and to find out information from our own government. This chapter will outline these expansions of the concept of free speech. It will also explain why certain important limits have been placed upon that freedom.

A Privilege or a Right?

When the English Parliament of 1593 begged Queen Elizabeth I to allow free debate in Parliament, she ruled that "Privilege of speech is granted, but . . . not to speak every one what he [wants], but your privilege is Aye or No."[2] That is not the American view. Here, free speech is not a privilege granted by the government, but a right protected by the government.

Just because a statement is allowed by the Constitution, however, does not mean it is guaranteed to be legal or wise. A person might defraud someone, ruin someone's reputation, or break a promise—and get sued or arrested for it. He or she will not be guilty, however, of violating the Constitution. The First Amendment limits the government more than it does individuals.

Forums for Speech

Free speech is guaranteed on one's own property. For example, in 1994 the Supreme Court struck down an ordinance that would have prohibited most signs on one's own property in a residential neighborhood.[3]

Second, in public places free speech will be protected:

> Wherever the title of streets and parks may rest, they have immemorially been held in trust for the use of the public and . . . have been used for purposes of assembly, communicating thoughts between citizens, and discussing public questions. Such use of the streets and public places has, from ancient times, been a part of the . . . liberties of citizens. . . .[4]

These places are called "public forums." Some electronic networks may also deserve that name. For example, public television networks can be public forums. *Not every public area is set aside as a forum, however.*

State-owned cemeteries, federal post offices, and county welfare offices have functions that do not lend themselves to marches and debates directly on the premises. Furthermore, a government can regulate the time, place, and manner of use of the people's public forums, but the forums must be open to all, without screening certain messages.

In other words, the rules must be "content neutral." The government may open up discussion on just one topic, as at a school board meeting. Yet once it does, the forum must be open to all viewpoints on that subject.[5] When it comes to privately owned but widely used property—such as apartment house bulletin boards, shopping center parking lots, and subsidized housing common areas—state constitutions and other laws may control content.[6]

What's Wrong With That Law?

The most common way that free-speech cases come to court is when a person does something that seems to violate a criminal law. In defending oneself, a person challenges the law under which he or she is being charged. For example, a person may claim that the law is "overbroad." That means that the law is worded so indefinitely that it outlaws at least some protected activity.

A law can also be vague; a law forbidding "insulting behavior" for instance, is too unclear. People have a wide variety of interpretations of insulting behavior, and two things might result—the people might avoid permissible activities simply because they do not know where the limits are or law enforcement officials might make inappropriate arrests by using their own opinions to come up with standards.[7] The courts disapprove of laws that give officials too much room in granting or denying free speech permits such as parade licenses.

In one recent case, the Supreme Court struck down the practice by a city official of charging different fees for different marches and event permits. Even though the Court accepted that the city almost always undercharged for crowd control and paperwork, "[t]he decision how much to charge for police protection or administrative time is left to the whim of the administrator."[8] That made it too tempting for officials to charge more for messages they did not like.

Finally, limits on speech must be "narrowly tailored" to serve an important governmental interest. They must leave open plenty of alternative channels for communication.

For example, a woman attempted to carry a picket sign along the sidewalk in front of the Supreme Court building and was prevented. She challenged the law that made it a crime "to parade, stand, or move in procession or assemblages in the Supreme Court Buildings or grounds." The Justices inside agreed

Americans are free to criticize their government, short of advocating its immediate violent overthrow. Here, Dr. Jack Kevorkian protests at a proceeding concerning physician-assisted suicide.

with her. They said that lawmakers had tried to destroy a public forum and had not "narrowly drawn" the law.[9] With this background we will now turn to specific examples of free speech.

Protected Protest

You turn on the radio; you scan the stations. On one, a man is being interviewed. He is complaining about the government's policies and how they affect him. Criticism of the government is the type of speech most fully protected by the First Amendment. Yet this right has had a rocky history.

Before the Constitution, colonial lawmakers came down hard on printers who spread criticism of the government. Even after the First Amendment was ratified, Congress passed the Alien and Sedition Acts. Under them, people could be severely punished for intentionally stirring up hatred for the government or making malicious, false statements about government officials.

The two main political parties at the time were called Federalists and Anti-Federalists (The Anti-Federalists were also known as Republicans, although they were not related to today's Republicans). The Anti-Federalists argued that the acts violated the First Amendment. The Federalists were first to gain the power under the laws. They used it against the Anti-Federalists. When the Anti-Federalists took over, however, they used it too. The acts were unpopular and soon died a welcome death. Fines levied under the Sedition Act were even repaid by an act of Congress.[10]

With the exception of some limits on speech during the Civil War, there was almost no congressional restriction on speech until World War I.[11] Under the

Espionage Act of 1917 and the Sedition Act of 1918, certain people were arrested for interfering with the war effort. One such case was *Schenck* v. *United States* in 1919, in which a Socialist party member and others had distributed leaflets that opposed the draft.[12]

Schenck did not dispute that his intent was to hinder the draft. He argued, however, that his speech was protected by the First Amendment. Justice Holmes appealed to "national security" interests. He wrote: "When a nation is at war, many things that might be said in time of peace are such a hindrance to its effort that their utterance will not be endured. . . ."[13] He stated that if speech raises a "clear and present danger" to lawful society, then speech and the press can be punishable.[14]

Later the Court upheld a conviction because a man had used "offensive and derisive names" for religion and for a police officer, which were "fighting words." The Court said:

> The lewd and obscene, the profane, the libelous, and the insulting or "fighting words" . . . are of such slight social value as a step to truth that any benefit that may be derived from them is clearly outweighed by the social interest in order and morality.[15]

More than twenty-five years after that came the case of *Brandenburg* v. *Ohio*. There, the leader of a Ku Klux Klan (KKK) group said that because the President, Congress, and the Supreme Court had, as he put it, conspired "to suppress the white, Caucasian race, it's possible that there might have to be some revengance [sic] taken."[16]

The Court concluded that only "incitements" to violence—urging imminent lawless action—were sufficient to overcome First Amendment guarantees. The

Court also held that the Ohio law under which Brandenburg was convicted could not be upheld.

Obscenity

Let us suppose that you tune your radio in to another station. On this one, you hear a comedian telling jokes that refer to sex. This same situation led to a Supreme Court case about what can be allowed on the airwaves. First, we will look at the background of obscenity laws in this country.

Until the mid-1800s, sexually explicit materials were seen mainly as threatening to religion. They were opposed more by churches and private groups than by government. The objectionable materials were limited to drawings and verbal materials. With the development of photography and mass printing, state governments began to be concerned.

In 1815, Vermont was the first state to outlaw the publication or distribution of obscene materials. Within thirty years almost all states had done so. With most laws forbidding only the publication of the material, free speech was not completely silenced. An individual acting privately was not covered by such laws. What we might call "hard-core obscenity" circulated to a small extent, but very secretly.[17]

The first cases on obscenity actually concern printed works that included questionable passages as part of a larger literary work. They include James Joyce's *Ulysses* and Theodore Dreiser's *An American Tragedy*. Of the latter book, the Supreme Court of Massachusetts warned that "[t]he seller of a book which contains passages offensive to the statute has no right to assume that children to whom the book might come would not read" them.[18]

Eventually, material with no apparent socially

redeeming content came before the courts. In *Roth* v. *United States* in 1957, the Supreme Court concluded that "obscenity is not within the area of constitutionally protected speech or press."[19] Later the Court held that a work is obscene if an average person applying community standards would find that overall it appeals to prurient interest (excessive interest in nudity, sex, or excretion), depicts sexual conduct in a patently offensive way, and that it lacks serious literary, artistic, political, or scientific value.[20]

If a work has some value, it can be protected as indecency, rather than obscenity, which is not protected. The fact that the work in question must be considered as a whole means that context is important—even the Bible discusses murder, rape, incest, and adultery. Context can also mean the time and place where the material might be encountered.

For example, we can note the radio broadcast in *FCC* v. *Pacifica Foundation* in 1978.[21] There, comedian George Carlin performed a monologue called "Seven Dirty Words." The monologue made fun of the Federal Communications Commission's (FCC's) list of seven words that would not be allowed in a broadcast.

A father driving with his child in the car heard it on his car radio. He was upset that this indecent material would come at them unexpectedly. Though he turned off the radio, he felt that harm had already been done. This led to the suit that eventually established that the FCC had the power to regulate speech on radio and television.

Cases on obscenity do not make heavy use of the word censorship. Censorship is best defined as "*government* limits on speech and the press." Censorship is not accurately applied to *private* parties who, by persuasive or commercial efforts such as boycotts, convince others to suppress materials.

For example, private entities such as a phone company or a television station are free to refuse to carry pornography or other objectionable materials, and the First Amendment is not violated.[22] In 1996 the Supreme Court held that cable television broadcasters could block "patently offensive" programs, noting that children were likely to be exposed to undesirable programs otherwise. The Court also ruled that cable operators had "editorial freedom" to block shows.

Politics and the Media

Next you tune in the radio to hear the voice of your mayor. He or she is making a campaign speech in a bid for reelection. The station may or may not carry a speech by the opponent.

In print media, the law even more clearly gives freedom to an editor to print only the stories he or she wants. In 1974 the state of Florida had a law that required newspapers to give free reply space to political candidates attacked by the papers. The Court unanimously held that this amounted to too much government tampering with the *editor's* free speech and free press rights.[23]

It would be nice to guarantee everyone the right to have his or her speech put into the newspaper, however, it is up to Americans to print their own statements or buy their own air time if it is not given to them. If a television station or newspaper is too biased, we expect the free market to produce a competitor who speaks for more people.[24]

If you hear or see an advertisement for a political candidate or about an election issue, someone paid for that ad. The law on contributions to campaigns has

Staunch conservative Rush Limbaugh's radio talk show prompted some people to promote the idea of a "Fairness Doctrine" to ensure that opponents have equal time on the air. Currently, this is not the law.

reversed itself quite a bit. Factors that the Court takes into account are whether the giver is a corporation, a political group, or an individual, and whether the money is given to an individual candidate or to influence the public on an issue.[25]

And Now a Word From Our Sponsor

The next station you hear on the radio is running a commercial for a pizza restaurant. Companies and individuals are allowed to use many different advertising techniques. They are not, however, free to lie about their competition. They can say that their pizza is the "best value" or the most delicious in town. They cannot, however, claim to be number one in pizza sales or have the most ingredients if that is false. This would amount to "libel," or false statement, about the competitor who really does have the most ingredients. Libelous speech is not protected by the Constitution. "Commercial speech," which invites a sale, is protected by the First Amendment, though to a slightly lesser extent than is other speech. For example, having parties to sell products, such as Amway™ or Tupperware™, on college campuses has been held not to be a protected activity.[26] It has also been ruled that cigarette advertising can be kept off any electronic media under the authority of the FCC, a government agency.[27] Gambling advertising can also be prohibited even where gambling is legal.[28]

Canvassing, or door-to-door sales, has led to several court decisions. Scholar Zechariah Chafee said:

> Of all the methods of spreading unpopular ideas . . . [door-to-door solicitation] seems the least entitled to extensive protection. The possibilities of persuasion are slight compared with the certainties of annoyance. [H]ome is one place where a man ought to be able to shut himself up in his own ideas if he desires.[29]

Yet the Supreme Court has refused to allow cities to ban religious and political canvassing, though they can limit it to day-time hours. Commercial canvassing, that is, door-to-door product selling, can be limited or forbidden.[30]

How Loud is Too Loud?

The next radio station you find is playing your favorite song. You enjoy it so much that you take your radio outside and turn up the volume. You are enjoying yourself so much that you do not notice your friend next door coming over until he is right beside you. "Please! Turn it down!" he says. "I'm trying to get some rest!" You go back inside, wondering how loud is too loud. Some people have taken that very question to court.

In *Ward* v. *Rock Against Racism* in 1989, the Supreme Court looked at a New York City ordinance that required all performers in the Central Park bandshell to use the sound amplification system and the sound technician that the city supplied. The Supreme Court held that the city had an interest in protecting its people from excessive noise, and that the regulation was a reasonable, "narrowly tailored" way to do this.[31] Most towns and cities have some ordinances that limit noise, especially during the late night and early morning hours.

The Arts

When you tune in the next station on your radio, a rap song is playing. Some of the words refer to violence. You question where the legal limits are when it comes to music or other communication that seems to support violence.

When shocking words or scenes appear in an artistic or religious context, they are almost always protected under the First Amendment. Exceptions occur when the artist is creating a danger to the public or committing a crime. For example, if a rock star hurts an animal as part of a show, he or she could be arrested under laws protecting animals from cruelty. One entertainer who reportedly was infected with HIV and performed by sticking himself and others with needles and by hanging paper towels that had blood on them out over the audience contributed to an outcry to withdraw taxpayer funding for the arts.[32] Such a controversial person may be forced to find private individuals and grants to fund him or her.

The Supreme Court has said that:

> A function of free speech . . . is to invite dispute. . . . [It] even stirs people to anger. . . . [But it is protected] unless shown likely to produce a clear and present danger . . . that rises far above public inconvenience, annoyance, or unrest.[33]

So-called "fighting words," which are threats or vicious insults in a face-to-face encounter, are not protected speech. Neither is "incitement to riot." Sometimes a speaker's words stir such reaction in a crowd that the best constitutional measure for the police is to arrest those reacting—not the speaker.

Symbolic Speech

Next you tune in the radio to a talk show. The host pounds on the desk next to his microphone as he makes his point. Certain actions are meant to communicate a message. Someone might pull on his ear to relieve a pain, but if he is a baseball pitcher it might mean, "Move in, team, I'm throwing my curve ball." Wearing certain clothing, sitting in a place where one is not supposed to, or placing flowers in a certain spot have all been means of expression and protest without words.

Take, for example, thirteen-year-old Mary Beth Tinker. She was a teen during the Vietnam War and wanted to speak out against the war. She and others decided to wear black armbands to school to take this stand. The school authorities felt that the armbands distracted from school activities and that disturbance might result from allowing the armbands. The authorities expelled her and others, but the Supreme Court recognized her action as speech, and said this:

> It can hardly be argued that either students or teachers shed their constitutional rights to freedom of speech or expression at the schoolhouse gate. . . .

> [U]ndifferentiated fear or apprehension of disturbance is not enough to overcome the right of freedom of expression.[34]

In a later case, a school became aware that some students were going to wear white armbands. Those students had threatened to tear the black armbands off their classmates' arms. That school's administration sensed "a rapidly developing crisis and prohibited all armbands."[35] The federal circuit court ruled that the prohibition was unconstitutional. One law text asks us to consider, "In a crisis situation, how many alternatives must be explored?"[36]

Despite its high ideals for student rights, the *Tinker* case has been limited somewhat. The action of burning a draft card to protest war was ruled not speech, but simply illegal conduct. A speech made by a high-school student at an assembly that contained sexual remarks was ruled not protected.[37]

Because our flag is a symbol, just about anything we do with it becomes a symbol too. In cases about using the flag in protest, the protester almost always wins. For instance, in *Texas* v. *Johnson* in 1989, Gregory Johnson burned an American flag at the Republican National Convention in Dallas in 1984. The state of Texas had a law stating that totally destroying a flag was conduct not protected under the Constitution. The Supreme Court rejected this, saying:

> [T]he government may not prohibit expression simply because it disagrees with the message. . . . We do not consecrate [honor] the flag by punishing its desecration, for in doing so we dilute the freedom that this cherished emblem represents.[38]

Americans have the free-speech right not to make statements that violate their conscience. This might include saluting the flag or other implied expressions.

In a recent case a private group was scheduling its annual St. Patrick's Day parade. The group was approached by the Irish-American Gay, Lesbian, and Bisexual Group of Boston to participate. The parade organizers refused to include them.

The Supreme Court held that the organizing group had a "right as a private speaker to shape its expression" and not give the new group a forum for expressing things that the original group did not approve.[39] In New Hampshire a man who disliked the motto on his car license plate reading "Live Free or Die" was allowed not to make such a statement—he had covered up that part of his plate.[40]

The Right to Know

You switch to one last radio station. You recognize the song from a great movie you saw last week. The movie was made from the book of the same name, and you wonder if the book is as good as the movie. You decide to find out.

The Constitution guarantees your right to go to the school or city library and check out books. (Unless you have too many overdue books—then the library has the right to protect its collection for others to use!) This is because the right to speak includes the right to know.

Through the years, various books have been so offensive to some people that those people sought to keep libraries from buying them, schools from teaching them, or students from reading them. The books range from love stories to political criticism to religious works such as the Bible and Salman Rushdie's anti-Muslim writings. The American Library Association (ALA), the American Civil Liberties Union (ACLU), and the Right to Read Foundation are three of the most vigorous defenders

James Madison (shown here) once said, "Knowledge will forever govern Ignorance: And a people who mean to be their own Governors, must arm themselves with the power which knowledge gives." Groups such as the ACLU believe that we should print as many opinions as possible so that people can make informed decisions.

of the right of anyone to read anything. Such groups say that librarians and publishers have a responsibility to "demonstrate that the answer to a bad book is a good one . . . [and to provide] diversity of thought and expression."[41]

However, even the most open-minded librarian has to make choices when he or she orders new books. All adults are also faced with making decisions about how tax dollars or tuition money should be spent. All young people are responsible for the choices they make about what to read. There is a distinct constitutional difference between people sorting through books on behalf of the state and people doing so for themselves or a private group.

For example, if you attend a private school or home school, your parents and teachers have no legal duty to give you access to a wide variety of books, especially if they consider them potentially harmful or unworthy of your time. A public institution, however, is controlled by the "equal protection" clause of the Constitution. The government must show an important reason for not including one voice among others.

Actions and records of public agencies are open to everyone under various state and federal laws such as the Freedom of Information Act of 1966. The freedom to keep an eye on our court system gives us a right to attend criminal trials. As a general rule, in noncriminal trials, all items filed with the court are public records.

Areas of controversy do exist, however. The right to uncover adoption records is in question, as is the amount of information that can be released about ongoing investigations. For example, police working to solve the murder of young Jon Benet Ramsey in

Colorado have been criticized for slowness in releasing information on what they are finding.[42] Should the public's curiosity be satisfied? Police sometimes want to keep secret certain details of a crime scene that might give away the offender's identity until after they have made an arrest. On the other hand, publishing some clues could allow the public to make a connection and perhaps suggest a suspect. For instance, an Ohio woman and her two daughters were brutally murdered while on vacation in another state. No suspects were uncovered for a year, until a note left by the killer was reprinted on area billboards. Within days, three people called in with identification of the writing. A suspect was convicted and sentenced to death.[43]

It is the public's right to know that protects people who file lawsuits, especially lawsuits that reveal that a business or institution is doing something wrong. Specific laws may prevent such businesses from taking revenge upon someone who "blows the whistle" on them. An act that contains some of these elements is descended from the Ku Klux Klan Act, or Civil Rights Act, of 1871. It outlaws conspiracy to do such things as threaten witnesses or jurors or to retaliate against them for their contributions to the judicial process.

The public's right to know propelled efforts to require nutritional information on food labels. It also requires government bodies such as school boards and city councils to post the times and places of their meetings as well as planned agendas so that the public can attend. It even figures in large policy decisions such as whether or not public funds will be used to provide abortion counseling to poor women.

In *Rust* v. *Sullivan* in 1991, the Supreme Court decided that the United States Department of Health and Human Services could forbid health care providers who received federal funds from telling women about abortion as a method of family planning or from referring the women to abortion providers.[44] This is a highly political issue. Related to this is the debate over when parents have a right to know that their children are receiving birth control, psychological counseling, or medical procedures.

> The scope of the constitutional right of privacy [such as that which surrounds a medical procedure] has never been clearly delineated. Nor has the Supreme Court ever held that the right of privacy prevails over the right to freedom of speech [such as a doctor's right to advise patients freely]. Nevertheless the issue is a recurring one and sooner or later . . . [a solution] will have to be formulated."[45]

The law is more clear on the right of parents to see their children's school records and to examine tests and instructional materials given to their children. Several federal laws provide for this.[46]

The freedom of speech is entwined with the other freedoms protected by the First Amendment. Especially important is the explanation of forums for speech in our chapter on the establishment of religion.

"Freedom of speech, as we have seen, is often afforded to those groups which [sic], if they were in power, would not be quite so generous with others."[47] But this is our answer to the question Lenin posed in Russia so long ago: "Shall we give a hearing to those who hate and despise freedom, to those who, if they had the power would destroy our institution? Certainly, yes! Our action must be guided, not by their principles, but by ours."[48]

3

Freedom of the Press

Imagine yourself in a quaint coffeehouse, relaxing by a fireplace as you browse through the events in the newspaper. You look up to see a friend drop in to buy a book. Is this a bookstore/coffee shop in a mall? No, this was the home of one of America's first newspapers in 1690. Benjamin Harris's *Publick Occurrences* was his venture into the local coffeehouse/bookshop/publishing business now occupied by companies such as Barnes and Noble™.

Some of the items in the little four-page paper raised questions about the government, however. The colonial authorities clamped down on the paper, and its first issue was its last. Before the American Revolution, such instances of censorship were common. Even telling the truth could get the colonial papers into trouble. The trial of a printer named Zenger established that truth was a defense to a charge of "seditious libel" (criticism of the government).

In 1765 British authorities went so far as to require that written matter had to appear on officially stamped paper. When the special paper was purchased, a tax would be added. The colonists found this "Stamp Act" infuriating. The authorities backed down within a year. Yet already "[t]he American press had been aroused and had become the champion of freedom and American patriotism."[1]

The press was a large part of the people's power to question and change their government and to find out about life in general. "We were one of the first peoples in the world to believe that we are entitled to know the whole truth about everything that interests us."[2] The Founding Fathers fiercely cherished the free press. Thomas Jefferson said, "Were it left to me to decide whether we should have a government without newspapers or newspapers without a government, I should not hesitate a moment to prefer the latter!"[3]

Of course, newspapers and television can be found in many nations. What they are allowed to say, however, varies widely. The differences rest in part on the guiding ideas of the paper. Many of our newspapers print on their front page their slogan or motto, stating their basic principle. It is commonly something such as, "And you shall know the truth, and the truth shall make you free" from the Bible, or Daniel Webster's "There is nothing so powerful as the truth."[4]

A Brief History of the Press

In the early years of our independence, many states allowed government officials to sue journalists for criticizing the government. Thomas Jefferson made noble statements about the freedom of the press, but when he suffered at its hands as President, he grumbled, "Nothing can now be believed which is seen in a newspaper. Truth itself becomes suspicious by being put into that polluted vehicle."[5]

Papers prior to approximately 1830 were mostly notices of ship arrivals and departures, reprints of news published elsewhere, editorials that were "strongly partisan, provocative, and ill-tempered" and advertisements.[6] Many newspapers were paid for by political parties or candidates.

By about 1830 "penny papers" began to be sold, not by subscription, but on the street by newsboys. These papers had to please average people on the street and the advertisers buying page space. In this way the cost of the paper could be kept low. Circulation quadrupled in ten years. In an effort to attract more readers and advertisers, some papers printed wild, unverified stories, gossip, and ridiculous ads. Novelist James Fenimore Cooper, author of *Last of the Mohicans*, complained:

> If newspapers are useful in overthrowing tyrants, it is only to establish a tyranny of their own. The press tyrannizes over publick [sic] men, letters, the arts, the stage, and even over private life. Under the pretence of protecting publick [sic] morals, it is corrupting them to the core. . . .[7]

Regardless of the poor quality of some of the papers, the press enjoyed a large degree of freedom and faced few legal challenges until almost the twentieth century. The American view of newspapers was for a long time embodied in Blackstone's *Commentaries* on law, first published in 1765:

> The liberty of the press is indeed essential to the nature of a free state; but this consists in laying no previous restraint upon publications, and not in freedom from censure for criminal matter when published. . . . [I]f [someone] publishes what is improper, mischievous, or illegal, he must take the consequences. . . .[8]

To this day, the "prior" or "previous restraint"

upon speech—that is, not allowing a manuscript even to be published—is a most serious offense against the Constitution. It is allowed *only* when publication of protected speech would create a major threat to national security.

The Post Office as Police

Interestingly, the United States Postal Service, as a department of the government, figured most often in early freedom-of-the-press disputes. In 1835 President Andrew Jackson asked Congress to prohibit the mailing of anti-slavery publications to southern states. This was during a time when slave owners feared that slaves would revolt. Senator Daniel Webster opposed the measure as a violation of the First Amendment.

During the Civil War thirty years later, the Postmaster General began removing pro-slavery material from the mail. Congress outlawed obscene material from the mail in 1865, and lottery materials were outlawed three years later. The Supreme Court ruled in 1892 that postal bans such as this were not censorship, since publishers were still left free to print the items.[9]

Later, four volumes of a magazine that printed parts of James Joyce's novel *Ulysses* were burned by the United States Postal Service as obscene. Before then, publishers had usually "self-censored." "They refused to publish books that might have offended the public taste."[10] For example, in 1890, *Century* magazine had "stopped the presses because of a reference to dynamite" in relation to labor troubles described in the novel *The Rise of Silas Lapham.*[11]

In 1946 the Supreme Court addressed the denial of a cheaper, "second-class" postage privilege to *Esquire* magazine. Losing this privilege would have cost the publication half a million dollars per year. The Court was concerned that postal officials would gain too much power to restrain free speech based on their own tastes. The power of post offices to deny their services remains, and the argument is that publishers or authors can distribute their materials some other way. Still, a post office never has the power to forbid the printing of any material.[12]

Sometimes a law is passed that attempts to do just that. It might prohibit publication of a category of material, such as "obscene, scandalous, or defamatory articles." Then if other people disapprove of the law, they can challenge the law in court and seek to have it struck down, since no law can violate the First Amendment.

This is what happened in the 1920s in Minnesota. Many "scandal sheets," outrageous gossipy newspapers, were appearing, and a "gag law" was passed to silence them. In 1927 the *Saturday Press* was served with a restraining order. It had used "racial slurs, called police 'rodents' and hurled incredible accusations at . . . local officials."[13] The *Press* demanded a hearing and the court eventually ruled in favor of the paper.

National Security

Another law that limited the mailing of printed material was the Espionage Act of 1917. It barred from the mails any publication that might cause disloyalty to the nation or obstruct the recruitment of soldiers during World War I. The 1918 Sedition Act banned favorable articles about nations at war with the United States. It also banned any disloyal, profane, or abusive language about the government. The laws were repealed a few years later. National security is a court-recognized interest that can override freedom of the press. This is only temporary, however. A famous case illustrates this.

During the Vietnam War, a former government official leaked some secret documents about the war to *The New York Times*. The paper then published a story on the information it received. The article touched off:

> one of the great constitutional struggles between press and the government. Here were forty-seven typescript volumes of secret government documents . . . and the *Times* had them all. [Then President] Richard M. Nixon didn't know the Pentagon Papers existed until [the story] was published. . . . But he knew he didn't like secrets [to appear printed] in the newspapers.[14]

Members of The New York Times composing room display a page containing excerpts from the Pentagon Papers. On June 30, 1971, the Supreme Court ruled that the paper had a right to print these controversial documents.

On the theory that confidential documents might endanger United States security, he had the Justice Department obtain a court order stopping publication of any more such information.

That same day, the *Washington Post* took up where the *Times* had left off. The Supreme Court eventually ruled that the "Pentagon Papers" could not be suppressed. The executive branch of the government (here, President Nixon) could stop the presses if it would avoid war or even chaos at home. The main purpose of the First Amendment, however, was to "prohibit the widespread practice of governmental suppression of embarrassing information."[15] In recent decades, freedom of the press has been an issue in several controversies. Lawsuits surrounding freedom of the press have continued.

Defamation

Defamation according to the law is "[a]n intentional false communication, either published or publicly spoken, that injures another's reputation or good name. . . ."[16] *The New York Times* was sued at one point for making such a statement about a public figure. In deciding the case, the Supreme Court designed a test for deciding whether a person who has "fame or notoriety" has been defamed.

The maker of the statement had to be acting out of actual malice, knowing that the statement was false or having reckless disregard as to its truth.[17] To show that a newspaper knew something is difficult to prove in court. The press rightly considered the Court's standard as very favorable toward them. Public figures, too, who attain fame although not elected, should also expect a wider array of things said of them in the press. Persons who are not famous can recover in court by showing, for example, that a statement about them invaded their privacy, kept them from getting a job, or broke up a relationship. They do not have to prove "malice."

Obscenity

Everyone involved in obscenity, from models and photographers to editors, publishers, and sellers of the material, can be and is prosecuted for obscenity-related crimes such as child abuse, various "public decency" laws, conspiracy or participation in rape, the delinquency of a minor, and distribution of pornography. A publisher can be named as a defendant in a criminal obscenity case, as in *Doubleday & Co.* v. *New York* in 1948.[18] The FCC can fine or even revoke the license of a broadcaster who shows "obscene, indecent, or profane broadcasts." The FCC does not have the authority to prevent a broadcast ahead of time. That would be an illegal prior restraint. The explosion of television channels available for broadcasting—from a handful twenty years ago to over fifty now—makes it virtually impossible for the FCC to monitor programming as closely as it once did.

The First Amendment has been ruled not to protect obscenity. It also does not protect material in which children are portrayed as engaging in sexual acts even if the poses do not quite amount to adult obscenity. This is because the children or teens who are forced or persuaded to be involved in these materials need the protection of the law. The adults around them cannot be counted on to act in the best interests of the young people.[19]

More and more, obscenity involves photos of torture and violence, and scenes that degrade women by making them appear to enjoy being victims.

Communication on the Internet is being found not just to transmit crude jokes or photos, but for dangerous adults to make contact with children, invite them to a meeting place, and make sexual or violent contact with them.

The Telecommunications Act of 1996 begins to address some of the issues, but with computer online services expected to be used by 170 million people by the year 2000 the freedom of speech and the press have merged together, and monitoring all of it for obscenity will be impossible.[20] Besides, who should get to be the monitor? In any case, America Online™, CompuServe™, and other services along with the ACLU and the American Library Association have filed suit to have the Telecommunications Act declared violative of free expression.[21] In June 1997, the Communications Decency Act (CDA), a specific section of the Telecommunications Act, was overturned.

Private persons and groups are free to combat businesses that sell obscenity by urging zoning restrictions and by picketing and boycotting such establishments.

Student Newspapers

What about the rights of students to publish what they want? Two cases outline those rights.

In *Hazelwood* v. *Kuhlmeier* a high-school journalism class presented the May 1983 issue of its paper to the school principal, as required.[22] The principal refused to allow two of the pages to be published, and three students on the paper's staff sued under the First Amendment. One of the articles in question featured some students who were pregnant, including details of their sexual conduct, and comments about the girls' parents. The principal, Robert Reynolds, said:

Students at Hazelwood East High School were not allowed to print this copy of their school newspaper, Spectrum, because of the content of some of the articles.

> It seemed obvious to me that the girls' parents had not consented to the story. . . . [T]wo of the articles contained information that might be libelous. . . . What's more, the article's upbeat tone wasn't my idea of balanced reporting. . . . [Reynolds was concerned with the article's] failure to address the kinds of long-term problems the girls might encounter. . . .[23]

Another article mentioned names of families in which the parents were divorcing, and referred to serious problems in the families such as alcoholism. "Identifying these families clearly violated their right of privacy," Reynolds felt.

> I didn't object to the articles because they dealt with controversial topics, but because they failed to meet

> our curriculum standards for responsible and ethical journalism. But . . . [i]f we held it up for rewrites, the journalism class wouldn't have time to publish the June issue.[24]

The Supreme Court decided in his favor that a journalism class must reflect the standards of the school.

> To teach teenage journalists that their First Amendment rights go beyond those of their adult counterparts is unrealistic, since if adult journalists can be sued for libel and invasion of privacy, school papers might be too.[25]

A more recent case also involved a student newspaper at the University of Virginia. The school required everyone to pay a small "student activity fee," pooled the money, and let the Student Council distribute it to student groups that were "related to the educational purpose of the University" including "student news, information, opinion . . . [and] media groups."[26] One of the groups that requested funds was a paper called *Wide Awake*. Its stated purpose was "to publish a magazine of philosophical and religious expression," and "to facilitate discussion which fosters . . . tolerance of Christian viewpoints."[27] Each page had a cross symbol on it, and the paper discussed various topics such as racism, pregnancy, free will, and music—all from a Christian perspective.

The university denied funding to the group. It claimed that promoting religion was not "related to the educational purpose" of the university. Since it was a state university, it had a concern that its funds not "establish," or fund, a religious publication, since the First Amendment seemed to forbid this in its Establishment Clause.

The Supreme Court struck down the denial. The Court reasoned that for the university to "cast disapproval on particular viewpoints of its students risks the suppression of free speech and creative inquiry in one of the vital centers for the nation's intellectual life, its college and university campuses."[28] The Court has consistently ruled that as long as a government agent, such as a university, allows discussion of certain topics, it cannot forbid discussion of those topics just because some people discuss the topics from a religious viewpoint.

The Right to Find Out

The freedom of members of the press and other media not just to publish but to obtain information is strengthened by two other rights—the freedom of the public to know (which is protected by the First Amendment as discussed in Chapter 2), and the right of the accused to a "public" trial.

Though at some events a "press pass" may get a reporter past a private gate, that is up to those in charge of the event, not the reporter. The press has no greater right of access to events under the First Amendment than you or I do. "The [Supreme] Court thus far has refused to draw any constitutional distinction between speech and the press, or . . . the 'organized media,' in part, perhaps, because there is no principled way of doing so."[29]

Who is exercising the "freedom of the press" right and not just the free-speech right to know that ordinary citizens have? What about someone who attends an event and wants to write an article about it but has no publisher? What about someone who prints a monthly newsletter on a laptop for a dozen friends? The Court is letting individuals decide such matters. The only significant laws in this area are in relation to coverage of criminal trials.

When it comes to news interviews with prisoners or press conferences held by prisoners, the Supreme Court has not found a positive right of the press to be present at these. "Newsmen have no constitutional right of access to prisons or their inmates beyond that afforded the general public."[30] Nor do they have a greater right to copy evidence offered in court or to attend a trial than the general public does. Where initial evidence could be televised and influence future jurors, "[i]n this area the rights of the press often conflict with the rights of the accused," since an accused has a due process right to an unbiased jury.[31]

Whether television cameras can enter a courtroom is up to state or federal law or the presiding judge, and opinions on the subject abound. For example, after the verdict in the trial of O.J. Simpson, Judge Lance Ito, who had presided over the trial, stated that he believed "the lawyers are pandering to the cameras." Steve Dunleavy, a journalist with the *New York Post*, said, "Since Biblical times, trials have always been public . . . All we're doing is making the room bigger . . . The cameras do nothing." On the other hand, columnist Richard Reeves said that television itself is "an environment" and that television would change trials as it has changed Congress, the presidency, and pro football.

Barry Scheck, a member of the Simpson defense team, said that much of the "instant analysis" that is so integral to television "is antithetical to the orderly unfolding of evidence." People should hear both sides of the facts before making up their minds. The father of Ronald Goldman, one of the victims, said that the trial had turned into "a pulpit for agendas." Craig Hume of KTLA-TV, which carried live gavel-to-gavel coverage of the trial, said his station was, indeed, encountering trouble from other judges getting cameras into other courtrooms.[32]

The press does have some privileges to guarantee that it can gather information even when some people do not want the information exposed. Most states have "shield" or "newsman's privilege" laws that ensure that a reporter will not be forced to reveal where he or she obtained information. However, in 1997, the Food Lion grocery chain of stores won a $5.5 million verdict against ABC News for a hidden-camera story that Food Lion said ABC got through deceptive tactics.

Getting on the Air

If you were to call your local televison or radio station right now and ask the manager to let you appear and tell the public something, the manager would probably tell you something like this: "Well, your ideas are very interesting, but unfortunately, we have only twenty hours a day to fit in our news, commercials, and entertainment; we just don't see a way to fit you in. Besides, you have to buy time, and for three minutes you would owe [several thousand dollars]." Even if you decided to start your own station, you would have to get a "broadcast frequency" and be licensed.

There is a limited amount of broadcasting wave frequency that can carry signals. We have given the government power to oversee radio and television because there is only a finite amount of transmitting frequency, which we all have to share. Since print media is not so limited, government does not make so many rules about who gets to use the newspapers (there is no real limitation on how many printers there are and how much paper they can produce). If you were running for class president and someone wrote a negative article against you, you could not force the newspaper to give you space in its paper to respond. Still most papers try to allow such "equal time," because it is fair and because it makes for more interesting reading.

Says scholar Owen Fiss:

> For the most part, the Free Speech Tradition can be understood as a protection of the street corner speaker. . . . But when our perspective shifts . . . from the street corner to, say, CBS, this [image of the street corner speaker] becomes highly problematic . . . CBS is not only a forum but also a speaker.[33]

He means that a large television network is not an open marketplace where everyone has a chance to speak, but rather it is a company steered by a few people who shape the whole message of their station. This company might not be interested in allowing air time to people who cannot pay for it, or people who have a different viewpoint than the television executives have.

While the American media may not be a perfect forum for all, it is an important force. With American radio and television spanning the globe, people everywhere are seeing us exercise our freedoms and are beginning to desire the same. CNN news anchor Bob Losure says:

> We're reaching a lot more people who never knew there was a First Amendment. The American press has contributed to the growth of democracy in the former Soviet Union and even the fall of the Berlin Wall. Global technology means free speech rights are spreading.[34]

4

An Establishment of Religion

It is the so-called Establishment Clause of the First Amendment that speaks on the issue of the relation of government to religion. It says that "Congress shall make no law respecting an establishment of religion." That is a simple statement, but it is one that is creating lots of emotion-filled debate today. It affects the school you are in, regardless of whether that is a public, private, or home school.

More than any other part of the First Amendment, the Establishment Clause demands that we understand the history surrounding its writing before we can hope to apply it today. As Thomas Jefferson said:

> On every question [of interpreting the Constitution], we must carry ourselves back to the time when the Constitution was adopted . . . and instead of trying what meaning may be squeezed out of the text . . . [take] the probable one in which it was passed.[1]

Some people say that our country was founded to escape religious persecution and to seek freedom. Others point out that the first colonies did not actually allow freedom, but were very rigid in their rules and beliefs, even setting up state-supported churches (called established religions). Which portrait of America is right? Both are.

Religious settlers came to this country hoping to set up communities where all agreed and shared the same lifestyle. Those who disagreed could start their own communities. Puritan Nathaniel Ward said that non-Puritans "shall have free liberty to keep away from us, and such as will come to be gone as fast as they can, the sooner the better."[2]

Not all of the early settlers, though, came with a religious purpose. Many were attracted to the New World to set up businesses and plantations. As more and more people moved in and shared resources, and as older communities changed and broke up, the towns and states no longer demanded to be identified by religious belief.

Once people of many faiths were living together, they saw the need to avoid letting one religion be the favorite of the emerging national government. The states that had established religions reconsidered the wisdom of having them. Still, disestablishing religion was the states' decision; it was not imposed by the Constitution. In theory, states kept their freedom to have established religions into the twentieth century.

The "leading architect" of the First Amendment, James Madison, originally wrote a draft of the First Amendment saying that no "*national religion*" (emphasis added) would be established. Thus the state religions were meant to be left alone. Nine of the thirteen original states of the Union had established religions. They certainly did not mean to make them illegal by passing a First Amendment.

For example, Maryland proposed a First

Amendment "That there be no national religion established by law."[3] Justice Joseph Story wrote that the framers of the Establishment Clause meant that ". . . the whole power over the subject of religion is left exclusively to the State governments, to be acted upon according to their own sense of justice and the State Constitutions."[4]

In 1947, the Supreme Court changed all of that in *Everson* v. *Board of Education.*[5] Americans, through Congress, had repeatedly voted down the idea. Still the Court applied the Establishment Clause to the states as well. Now such varied bodies as state prisons, welfare systems, public schools, and city parks and libraries are required by law to avoid "establishing" a religion.

So what does it mean to establish a religion? The New York convention that considered the First Amendment suggested this wording: "[N]o religious sect or society ought to be favored or established by law in preference to others."[6] Other states echoed this. James Madison summarized their efforts this way:

> . . . Congress should not establish a religion, and *enforce the legal observation of it by law* [emphasis added]. . . . [T]o prevent these effects . . . the amendment was intended, and . . . was as well expressed as the nature of the language would admit.[7]

That is, the First Amendment was intended to keep Congress from passing a law saying that "all citizens must be baptized as Catholics," or "Jewish people must pay twice the taxes of everyone else."

On the other hand, the writings of the framers show that the Establishment Clause did not, for them, mean that religion could have no influence in the public square. The following quotes illustrate the prevailing attitude of the time:

"The moral principles . . . contained in the Scriptures ought to form the basis of all our civil constitutions and laws."[8]

—Noah Webster, fighter in Revolution, ratifier of Constitution, judge

"It cannot be emphasized too strongly or too often that this great nation was founded, not by religionists, but by Christians; not on religions, but on the gospel of Jesus Christ!"[9]

—Patrick Henry, revolutionary and driving force behind adoption of the Bill of Rights

"[E]ducation should teach the precepts of religion, and the duties of man towards God."[10]

—Gouverneur Morris, United States Senator who actually wrote down the Constitution

"It is impossible to rightly govern the world without God and the Bible."[11]

—George Washington, first President and Chairman of the Constitutional Convention

"God grant that in America true religion and civil liberty may be inseparable . . ."[12]

—John Witherspoon, who signed the Declaration of Independence and served on over one hundred Congressional Committees

Not only the words but also the actions of the Founding Fathers give us a clue to their interpretation of the First Amendment. The day after they ratified it, they passed a resolution urging that people fast and pray to "Almighty God." In fact, the two Presidents who were at the Constitutional Convention and the President who wrote the first draft of the First Amendment all issued Thanksgiving prayer proclamations.[13] One of the earliest acts of the first

House of Representatives was electing and funding a chaplain—a minister selected to assist members of Congress in spiritual matters, a post that continues to this day. James Madison was a member of the committee that recommended this post.

The first eight Congresses gave money to Christian groups for teaching Native Americans and "promoting Christianity" among them.[14] Six Presidents, including Jefferson and Washington, signed treaties with Native Americans that paid for churches and other religious aid to Native Americans.[15] Jefferson, while President, was also the first president of the Washington, D.C., public school board, which used the Bible and a hymnal as the reading texts in all classrooms. This was not some oversight by him; he wrote, "I have always said, and will always say, that the [careful study] of the sacred volume [the Bible] will make us better citizens."[16]

In fact, in the 1700s and 1800s, public school students learned the alphabet by memorizing a Bible verse that began with each letter. As late as the 1960s, schools taught the Bible as basic truth and as the highest guide for conduct. Public schools no longer do this, and public bodies rarely say or do the types of things listed previously. What caused the change?

One cause was a line of Supreme Court decisions between about 1945 and 1980 that broke with the long line of cases before, which had applied the Establishment Clause. During the years before, the Supreme Court had consistently called us a "Christian nation" and rarely found Establishment Clause violations.[17] This was partly because it was thought that federal government was the only form of government that was forbidden to establish religion, since the Establishment Clause says only that the federal

"*Congress* [emphasis added] shall make no law . . ." establishing religion.

In the 1947 *Everson* decision, the Supreme Court broke this tradition and held that cities and states might also be guilty of activities that served to establish religion. While *Everson* itself held that busing to private schools did not violate the Establishment Clause, the Court began to find many city and state government activities that did. *Engel* v. *Vitale* in 1962, for example, eliminated spoken prayer in public schools even when it was voluntary. The next year *School District of Abington Township* v. *Schempp* banned Bible readings conducted by school staff. *Stone* v. *Graham* went on to find, in 1980, that posting the Ten Commandments in public schools was also a violation of the Establishment Clause.

None of these cases cited any precedent or case history from any time before 1947. *Committee for Public Education* v. *Nyquist* only relied on one case before 1947, while it referred to ninety-nine cases in or after 1947. *Nyquist* struck down tax-funded repairs at private schools. *Marsh* v. *Chambers* in 1982 ruled in part against a state chaplaincy program. Justices turned to only one case written before 1947 and thirty-two cases after 1947 in issuing their opinion. The Court, by making the Establishment Clause applicable to the states and cities, wrote quite a bit of new law.

In more recent years the Supreme Court has returned to earlier historical sources in order to interpret what the Establishment Clause means. Justice William Rehnquist's dissenting opinion in *Wallace* v. *Jaffree* and Justice Clarence Thomas's thorough history in *Rosenberger* v. *University of Virginia* show that the Court has not forgotten its past.

Is it true that the early documents claim that there is a "wall of separation" between church and state? The phrase does not appear in the Constitution, or anywhere else in early law. Twelve years after the First Amendment was ratified, Thomas Jefferson used the phrase in a letter he wrote to a Baptist organization. In it he was echoing a Baptist document that speaks of God building a "hedge or wall of separation between the garden of the church and the wilderness of the world" to protect the church.[18] Elsewhere he said: "I consider the government of the United States as [prohibited] by the Constitution from meddling with religious institutions. . . ."[19]

The Supreme Court's own rulings, as well as Congress's and the President's own actions have shown that the phrase "separation of church and state" is probably not a very useful one, since it is so full of exceptions. As one scholar says, "it suggests more questions than it answers."[20] It is more useful to ask whether government appears to be favoring one belief or nonbelief over another, whether it is forcing religious belief on a person, or whether it is forcing people with their taxes to pay for religious activity.

The Establishment Clause seems only to forbid Congress from making certain laws. In the last fifty years, however, the clause has also been held to apply to all kinds of public (tax-supported) groups and agencies. It is easier to understand the cases discussed here and in the chapter on free exercise of religion if one remembers whether a public, or government-related, entity is involved. A private group or individual has complete freedom to make religious or anti-religious statements; if a government-related body is involved and appears to hold or force on others a particular religion or anti-religious view, it will be offending the

The legislative and judicial branches of our government are often at odds over how to interpret the First Amendment. U.S. Representative J.C. Watts is critical of the Supreme Court's doctrine of separation of church and state.

Establishment Clause by in effect establishing a state religion.

For example, a public school may not teach Bible or Koran classes on its campus. Nor may students leave a public school to take such a class from a private teacher during the school day.[21] However, the Court has often allowed state religious expressions if they are historically or culturally based or they are the statements of government officials expressing their own faith. Here are some examples of the Court's analysis.

In *Lemon* v. *Kurtzman* in 1971, Chief Justice Warren Burger assaulted the "wall of separation," saying that "[T]he line of separation, far from being a 'wall,' is a blurred, indistinct, and variable barrier depending on all the circumstances of a particular relationship."[22] In a case about whether a state could help fund teacher pay and textbooks for church schools, he and the rest of the Court fashioned a test now called the *Lemon* test for deciding establishment clause cases: Does the action in question:

- have only a religious purpose?
- mainly serve to either advance or inhibit religion?
- call for a lot of government "entanglement" in religion?

If so, it fails the *Lemon* test, and therefore establishes a religion. (In the *Lemon* case itself, the Supreme Court found entanglement, which doomed the funding.)

Therefore, if a city passed an ordinance requiring people to recite a prayer to Allah before they could receive welfare benefits, that would fail the first two questions, and thus, violate the Establishment Clause. Forcing people to say a prayer would have no secular (nonreligious) purpose and would serve to promote

Islam. If a court took a case in which a church congregation sued its leadership over whether to baptize its members by dunking or sprinkling them, that would entangle the state in religious matters in which it has no jurisdiction or expert opinion. These are simple, extreme examples, but they illustrate the use of the *Lemon* test. The test has led to quite a variety of results, many of which seem at odds with each other. Some lawyers and judges dislike the test.

In *Lynch* v. *Donnelly*, a city and its merchants had placed a nativity scene in a city park. This Christmas display included the baby Jesus in a manger, along with other traditional figures. The Court ruled that this was allowable.[23] The most recent case involved a cross placed with permission by a private group near an Ohio statehouse lawn. It was a public area where a variety of both religious and nonreligious symbols had been displayed. The Court allowed the cross, but the Justices did not produce a majority opinion on the test to apply when a private group seeks to place a religious symbol on public property.

Justice Sandra Day O'Connor repeated her commonsense approach of asking whether a reasonable observer would take the display as an endorsement of religion. Justice David Souter wrote favorably of putting up a disclaimer or notice that the government does not mean to force a belief on people with the display.[24] The case law that encourages mixing religious with nonreligious symbols is good-humoredly called "the plastic reindeer rule." A religious object can be displayed in a cultural context or if there is no nonreligious substitute for it, such as the Court has said is the case with a Hannukah menorah.

Religious activities taking place on public property have given rise to many Establishment Clause cases.

Private speech on public property can make the government appear to be the speaker at times. Problems all over the country arose with public libraries, parks, and schools being used for such things as showing religious films, studying the Bible, and praying. The Supreme Court addressed these questions in *Lamb's Chapel* v. *Center Moriches*. The Court unanimously held that a school that opened its auditorium after hours for programs on topics such as family, health, artistic, and community concerns, had to allow a film series by psychologist Dr. James Dobson, advocating a return to Christian family values. To do so was not to establish a religion, but merely to be fair and not discriminate against a religious viewpoint.[25] This is the "forum analysis" that is discussed in the chapter on free exercise of religion: If a forum, or place for public debate, is opened, then a religious viewpoint must be allowed.

Another example of a seeming exception to the Establishment Clause is found in the controversy over the use of religious symbols in government seals and symbols such as state crests, flags, stamps, oaths, and money. The ACLU, a longtime opponent of such government symbols, often takes cases on the subject. Cities and states have lost some of their battles to keep such symbols, but the United States, or federal government, has consistently rejected attempts to change the Pledge of Allegiance and our dollar bills and coins, which say, "In God We Trust." The reason usually given is that these tokens of a religious heritage do not threaten our freedom to believe as we wish.

A recent surprising turn of events led to another exception to the Establishment Clause. The Supreme Court reopened a case that it had decided about twelve years before, and came to a different result. Taxes paid to public school teachers who assist disabled students in private schools were held not to offend the Establishment Clause. The Court seems to be allowing more interaction between public and religious institutions.[26]

A final example of exceptions to the Establishment Clause is personal statements made by government officials. Prayers to a Judeo-Christian God have been

Madalyn Murray O'Hair, an atheist who successfully fought school-led prayer, is shown here with her attorney. An atheist is one who denies the existence of God.

offered at presidential and state governor inaugurations from the first days of the nation. In times of crisis, government leaders commonly call upon the people of America to pray.

These situations do not seem to give rise to lawsuits. Recently President Bill Clinton wrote to a congressman to explain why the President would veto a particular bill. He wrote that he had studied and prayed about it a great deal.[27]

The law basically attempts to avoid hostility toward any belief system and to be neutral in its treatment of those who believe and of those who do not. This is consistent with the intent of the Founding Fathers. Madison wrote, "Who does not see that the same authority which can establish Christianity, in exclusion of all other Religions, may establish with the same ease any particular sect of Christians, in exclusion of all other Sects?"[28] What kept the Founding Fathers from persecuting non-Christians was actually their own religious faith, which caused them to believe that no one should be forced to agree with them. As Patrick Henry said:

> [Our religion] can be directed only by reason and conviction, not by force or violence; and therefore all men are equally entitled to the free exercise of religion, according to the dictates of conscience; and that it is the mutual duty of all to practice Christian forbearance, love, and charity towards each other.[29]

With the wide variety of beliefs in our nation now, the courts have fashioned limits on the government that will protect us from state religion.

5

Free Exercise of Religion

"Congress shall make no law . . . prohibiting the free exercise [of religion]."

If this book makes only one thing clear, it should be that the First Amendment controls government activities much more than it does private activities of individuals. The law requires that all levels of government accommodate a variety of religious beliefs:

In the public schools:

> When the state encourages religious instruction or cooperation with religious authorities by adjusting the schedule of public events to [religious] needs, it follows the best of our traditions. For it then respects the religious nature of our people and accommodates the public service to their spiritual needs.[1]

In the workplace: Workers cannot be discriminated against because of their religion:

> The term "religion" includes all aspects of religious observance and practice, as well as belief, unless an

> employer . . . is unable to reasonably accommodate to an employee's . . . religious observance or practice without undue hardship . . . on the business.[2]

Here are some instances of accommodation of a student's or worker's religion:

- *Children are allowed to leave campus during school hours for religious instruction (conducted by nonschool leaders), in some cases getting forms of credit for their work.*

- *A hospital worker is allowed to wear a turban; a mine worker is not because he or she must wear a hard hat to be safe (but perhaps he could be transferred to an office).*

- *A woman applying for a firefighter's job refuses to work on Sundays—this might not be accommodated because it could force her to leave in the middle of her task or force others to work double shifts; a librarian refuses to work on Saturdays due to his need to observe his Sabbath, or holy day of rest—this probably could be accomodated.*

Notice that it is the government that must accommodate and act neutrally toward religious exercise. Private (non-tax-supported) companies, private schools, and religious institutions need not accommodate religious views with which they do not agree. An interesting problem faces us when a private organization is so big and has so much control over people that it basically acts much like a government in terms of how much it controls people.

Several cases have examined the right to pass out literature or "witness" about one's faith in shopping malls. Most malls are owned and operated by private companies. They often serve some of the purposes, however, as the old town square where people gathered to talk and do business. Airports and fairgrounds are also desirable places for those who want to communicate their views. Again, such places are often held by private organizations. The law has given these private bodies a duty to allow some free expression.

In the so-called *Jews for Jesus* case in 1987, the Supreme Court found that no public facility in the area served the purposes that the private airport did, so the Court struck down the airport's overly broad rule against "First Amendment activities."[3]

Malls have been given a little more choice about whom to allow to speak, because the courts recognize that they must maintain an atmosphere that is not threatening and will encourage people to linger and shop. At fairs, all kinds of groups are usually permitted to have booths. They may, however, be forbidden to roam the grounds seeking converts to their views. Here the state's compelling interest in crowd control and safety is valid.[4]

When a company has fifteen or more employees, the Equal Employment Opportunity Commission (EEOC) oversees how the company treats its employees to make sure there is no discrimination against religious persons.

Everyone agrees that Americans have total liberty of thoughts in regard to religion—this is often called "freedom of conscience." Such beliefs do not just exist in the thought realm, however. They also exist in our words and actions. As one civil rights lawyer pointed out, "It's not the free belief clause—it's the free *exercise* clause."[5]

But, in one early case, a religious group practiced bigamy—the marriage of a person to more than one spouse at once. This practice was illegal under state laws and was held not protected by the Free Exercise

Clause. The practice, not the beliefs surrounding it, was being regulated. "[T]he legislative powers of the government," wrote Thomas Jefferson, "reach actions only, and not opinions."[6]

It is part of human nature for people who believe something to talk about it and want others to agree with them. The Supreme Court has consistently stood on the side of those who try to convince others of their beliefs. The Court has commented that the Constitution does not only protect unsuccessful attempts to persuade. "It would be a barren marketplace of ideas," Justice William Brennan once wrote, "that had only sellers and no buyers."[7] One case will illustrate.

Jesse Cantwell was a member of the Jehovah's Witnesses. He once approached two people on the street in a predominantly Catholic neighborhood and asked if they would listen to a recording. They agreed to do it. The record described a book titled *Enemies* and attacked other religions, including Catholicism. The listeners were offended, and Cantwell was prosecuted for creating a disturbance. However, the Supreme Court noted that Cantwell was not noisy or overbearing, and that "he wished only to interest [others] in his propaganda."[8] In such a case, the state of Connecticut had to find a "clear and present danger to a substantial interest of the State" before it could punish Cantwell. The Court allowed the state to regulate the time, place, and manner of such speech in a nondiscriminatory way, but not to outlaw it.[9] This was not a free speech case—it is a case protecting the free exercise of religion.

Regulating free exercise has been a complicated matter for American government. Young people may avoid going to combat because their religious beliefs

Thomas Jefferson said, "God almighty hath created the mind free." Jefferson believed that laws should regulate actions but never opinions.

forbid killing, but they may be drafted for some other area of public service. Parents who believe in using prayer rather than medical care to treat illness may have a critically ill child taken from them, depending on what local law requires. Schools have sometimes adopted "zero-tolerance" policies forbidding gang-related jewelry or clothing, only to find that rosaries on the ceremonial knife carried by Sikhs are demanded by religious custom.[10]

President Bill Clinton issued guidelines in 1995 through the United States Department of Education. The guidelines explained to public schools that students may express their religious ideas any time when they may express nonreligious ideas. When they have free time on campus, they may pray individually or in groups, pass out religious literature, or read scriptures of their faith. In assignments they may express faith or question it. Teachers and textbooks may discuss religion and encourage classroom discussion of the contributions that faith has made to our society and history.[11] Though all issues are not settled, voluntary student-led prayers at events such as graduations and football games are usually allowed and cannot be edited for religious content by a school. Samuel Adams is called the Father of the American Revolution. He served in Congress until 1781 and was once asked if the wide variety of faiths in America presented a problem for Congress having a chaplain and opening in prayer. He said, "I am not a bigot. I can hear a prayer from a man of piety and virtue, who is at the same time a friend of his country."[12]

A final case will explain free-exercise law in a school setting. Bridget Mergens, a high school student, wanted to meet with other students to study the Bible at a time during the school day when other

Often it is up to the Justices of the Supreme Court to define what is protected or unprotected under the First Amendment. From left to right standing are: Ruth Bader Ginsburg, David Souter, Clarence Thomas, and Stephen Breyer. Seated from left to right are: Antonin Scalia, John Paul Stevens, William Rehnquist (Chief Justice), Sandra Day O'Connor, and Anthony Kennedy.

clubs met. Her principal said no. Eventually she had to sue to establish that she had that right under a law that Congress had passed, called the Equal Access Act. The Supreme Court ruled that the act did not establish religion. Justice Sandra Day O'Connor used an analysis of the "limited open forum."

If a public secondary school opens a "forum" for speech, it cannot forbid religious speech. If clubs are allowed that do not have to do with a certain class, then a student-initiated religious club has to be allowed. It has to be allowed access to bulletin boards, the public address system, and other means of recruitment of members just like other clubs have. A public faculty member can attend to ensure discipline if that is required of other meetings, but the faculty member should not direct the meeting.[13] The *Mergens* reasoning has now been extended to the use of a school building after hours to show religious films and library meeting rooms used for Bible study.

A debate that may go to the Supreme Court in the near future concerns the free-exercise rights of landlords. The same situation has come before several courts where a landlord who, because of sincerely held religious beliefs, does not approve of certain tenants, such as unmarried or homosexual couples. Does the landlord have the free-exercise right to refuse such tenants? Massachusetts, Wisconsin, and other states have said yes; California said no in the spring of 1996. When the highest courts of various states disagree, the Supreme Court will often accept a case in order to make the law uniform throughout the country.

Another case that may wind up in the Supreme Court would involve the free-exercise rights of parents. The Court has been fairly sympathetic to the rights of religious parents to raise their children as they see fit. In *Wisconsin* v. *Yoder*, the Court granted Amish parents the right to keep their children out of state-run schools.[14]

In *Pierce* v. *Society of Sisters*, the Court said, "The child is not the mere creature of the State . . . ," and struck down a requirement that all students above eight years of age had to be in public school.[15] Congress protected the family's privacy with the Hatch Act, which allows parents to refuse certain kinds of testing of their children.

Home schooling is now legal in every state, with

perhaps as many as a million students learning at home.[16] More controversies keep rising, however. Can home-schooled children be barred from public school athletic programs? When can a public school student opt out of sex education or other classes that he or she finds offensive? What rights of religious "free exercise" do elementary school students have—or students who say they have no religion?

These questions remain either unanswered or answered in conflicting ways. Some people are arguing for a Religious Equality Amendment to the Constitution, which they hope would remedy some of the seeming injustices. Others suggest that a law or amendment that makes clear that Congress never intended the Establishment Clause to apply to the states would wipe out the *Everson* line of cases, allowing greater free exercise of religion. Yet it is doubtful that such an amendment would stop Americans from debating the place of religion in public life. The vigorousness of the debate indicates that Americans care very deeply about their freedom to believe (or not believe) and act without government interference.

6

Freedom of Assembly and Petition

The right of assembly means the right to get together with other people. The right of petition for redress means the right to seek improvements in our government. The two concepts are often linked, because we often need each other's help to make protests known to those in power. The Supreme Court recognized this in *NAACP* v. *Patterson* when it observed that promoting new ideas, "particularly controversial ones, is undeniably enhanced by group association."[1]

People need each other's support and abilities to do things such as publish newsletters, get media attention, and take their cases to court if need be. Alexis de Tocqueville was a French political observer of our early constitutional life. He said in 1835 that the United States more than any other country cherished "the principle of association."[2] Gathering with others is usually crucial to the exercise of any First Amendment right.

The Freedom of Assembly Clause in the First Amendment allows for people to form groups that will help them to spread their opinion or cause. For example, people come together to add to the AIDS quilt, which memorializes those who have died of the disease. Ryan White, who contracted HIV as a child, is remembered here.

Freedom to Associate

Freedom of association ensures that a government cannot intrude upon family relationships. The Supreme Court has often looked at the family as a "buffer between the individual and the state."[3] A child cannot be pulled from his or her home unless the authorities can show a court that abuse is occurring. When people leave wills or set up trusts on the condition that the receiver be a racist or never marry, such a condition may not be enforced because people have to be allowed freedom to marry and to associate with each other.[4] Freedom of association could also be an argument in favor of homosexual marriage. However, the Supreme Court has, thus far, upheld laws outlawing homosexual acts. The debate over this issue will be difficult to settle.[5]

People in this country are permitted to work together to picket, file lawsuits against the government, form new political parties, and do anything that is not a criminal act or the planning of a criminal act. For instance, when high school students and others were arrested for picketing schools in protest of racial discrimination, the Court said their cities' laws against picketing were too restrictive. "[G]overnment may not prohibit others from assembling or speaking on the basis of what they intend to say."[6]

The right to associate freely is not threatened only by police breaking up a gathering. It can also be threatened when the government wants to know about a group's membership or when it spies on its meetings. In hearings on unofficial military groups (private "militias") held in the summer of 1995, one congressman asked a militia member not accused of any crime to furnish his militia membership list. The member refused. While it was not illegal for the congressman to ask, it was not illegal for the member to refuse.[7]

Another threat to free association is the requirement that people reveal all their prior activities and memberships before they can serve in government. Even the oaths taken by candidates or newly elected officials must be narrow in scope and usually limited to a promise to uphold constitutional processes.[8]

People who want to work for the government usually cannot be denied on the basis of their political affiliation, unless their political group is working toward the violent overthrow of the government. Close associates of elected officials can be chosen on

A man with a bullhorn addresses a large audience. The First Amendment allows for people to meet, discuss, and spread their ideas.

the basis of their politics, however; otherwise they may not work effectively with their boss.

Freedom Not to Associate

Implied in the freedom of association is the freedom *not* to associate. That is, the government may not force us to be with or be identified with those with whom we do not wish to associate. For example, when teachers work for a school, they may band together into a union, a group that represents them in any conflicts with the school. Yet sometimes teachers feel that the dues they paid to get into the union are not being spent on their concerns. On the basis of freedom not to associate, the Supreme Court has protected teachers who do not want their union dues to be used for causes that are unrelated to union matters.[9]

However, the government may step in and limit the freedom of association. One limit is the fact that reasonable "time, place, and manner" restrictions can be imposed on gatherings. Eighty people do not have a constitutional right to have a noisy party in an apartment at 2:00 A.M. One of the most notable examples is in cases where men have barred women from clubs that appear merely social, but which, in fact, are very helpful in networking for business contacts and influencing others. In cases concerning the Jaycees and Rotary Clubs, the Supreme Court has said that any argument for such male-only networking "was outweighed by society's interest in equal treatment of men and women."[10]

Petitioning for Redress

The right to petition is observed in many different activities. For example, people still gather names on petitions. One recent effort has been to pass laws on term limits—how long an elected official can serve. People seem to continue to find many creative and peaceful ways to let our leaders know what we are thinking. Candlelight vigils in protest of the death penalty may be held outside a prison where an inmate is to be executed. Pro-life and pro-choice protesters have used various means of protest in their continuing battle over the issue of abortion.

One of the most dramatic petitions to Congress protested a bill that some thought endangered private school and home-school teachers. Lawmakers were swamped with so many calls and faxes—over eight hundred thousand—that on February 22, 1994, a number of them asked their staff to stop answering the phone.[11] Thanks to technology and creativity, we have many ways to seek change in our government.

A Liberty Tree for All

It should be remembered that the First Amendment was drafted by men who had lived as subjects to a king they felt was cruel and unwilling to change things. They tried hard to bring about change, but the royal government would not listen to them. As Thomas Jefferson put it in the Declaration of Independence, "[W]e have petitioned for redress in the most humble terms: Our repeated petitions have been answered only by repeated injury." So when it was time to begin a new nation, these men made sure that people could have peaceful channels for making improvements in their government with no fear.

An early expression of Americans' love of their freedom to associate is the Liberty Tree. In 1765, near Boston Common, a protest against England took place at a large elm tree. The group that gathered became known as the Sons of Liberty. In New York the Sons of

Liberty erected a large mast or pole as their gathering point; the British cut it down. The Sons put it back up. Fights broke out. ". . . [I]t became almost a contest between the British troops and the New York Sons of Liberty whether or not the pole should stand."[12]

Later others used the poles for their protests. The poles were found as far south as Savannah, Georgia. One witness said the Liberty Poles ran "in grand colonnade from the banks of the Delaware to those of the Susquehanna."[13] They were even lifted up in protest against slavery. The First Amendment is now our Liberty Tree—a rallying point where we can gather to call for change.

7

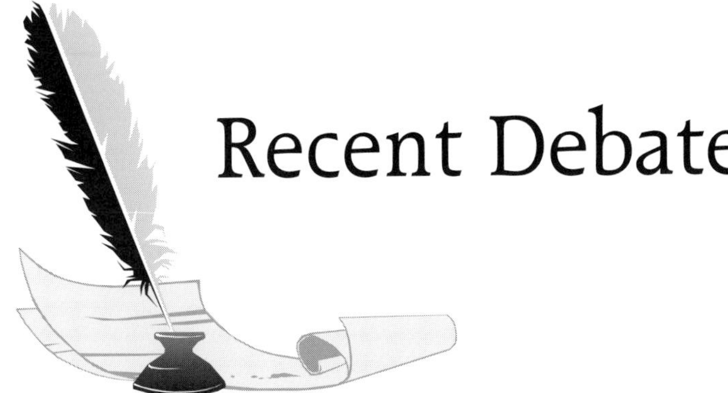

Recent Debate

Controversy still surrounds many First Amendment issues: Should religious medical students be required to learn how to do abortion procedures? Should students be able to lead others in prayer at a school event? What are the free speech rights of teachers? How far can joking in the workplace go without being "sexual harassment"? All of these issues and more are discussed daily on television and in current magazines and online services. Let us examine three recent cases.

- The United States Supreme Court recently examined free-speech rights of abortion protesters. In *Schenck* v. *Pro-Choice Network*, a "floating bubble zone" had been created around patrons and staff of an abortion clinic.[1] This meant that abortion protestors would have to keep a certain distance away from these people at all times. The Court ruled that a "fixed" zone around clinic entrances was allowable, but that an additional "floating" zone around people going in and out of the clinic was a violation of protesters' free speech.

- Mr. Keen Umbehr was a trash hauler for a county in Kansas, under contract with the County Board. Umbehr became an outspoken critic of the board, writing letters to the local newspaper and campaigning to become a board member. The board terminated its contract with him and he sued, claiming he was retaliated against for his

A group of young women is staging a peaceful protest against abortion. In 1996, the Justices of the Supreme Court heard oral arguments regarding whether a fifteen-foot "floating bubble zone" protecting clients and staff at abortion clinics from unwanted communication violated the free-speech rights of abortion protestors.

views. The Supreme Court agreed, refusing to allow "the government's disagreement with certain political expression."[2]

- Several teenagers in St. Paul, Minnesota, gathered one summer night and assembled a cross out of tape and broken chair legs. Then, these white teens entered the fenced yard of a black family nearby and burned the cross. The city prosecuted one of the teens under its "hate-crime law," which the teen's attorney claimed was unconstitutional. The attorney said it was "overbroad." In other words, it prohibited some lawful speech solely on the basis of the subjects the speech covered. The Supreme Court agreed.

The Court did not, however, make a statement, take a position, or otherwise decide on what the teens did. The Court was not asked to prosecute the teens, but to apply the Constitution to a law to see if the law was written correctly. The Court held that it was not. Unfortunately the Court's opinion is very difficult to understand. One Justice wrote, "The decision is mischievous at best and will surely confuse the lower courts," and refers to "the folly of the opinion."[3] Another said that other Justices were involved in "word-play."[4] This case, called *R.A.V.* v. *St. Paul*, shows us that attempting to control "hate crime" with laws is going to be difficult to do.

One newspaper article about hate speech suggests a different approach, which is typically American:

> The more we call out the names of the respectable people who are supporting racist speech, the more we boycott them and the racistspeakers, and the more we speak out against racist speech, the more we will stop racist speech. And we, the people, should do it with as little as possible of the heavy hand of the government.

> Boycotts are a legitimate answer to bad speech, and a much less dangerous answer than opening the door to censorship by government.[5]

New developments are not limited to the courts. In August of 1997, President Bill Clinton issued guidelines for businesses, assuring that their employees will have religious freedom in the workplace.[6]

In the future, one of the hottest areas of law will be school-related. "This is the single largest category of calls we get," said Rita Woltz, legal coordinator for a national civil liberties organization.[7] Lawmakers and judges will be deciding on such matters as whether allowing taxpaying parents a tuition break at a private school is an establishment of religion. The current trend seems to favor allowing such "vouchers." Lawmakers and judges will also consider how much schools can limit the expressive freedom of students and teachers and the freedom of parents to have input into public education.[8]

Young people can expect to see many new dilemmas relating to the First Amendment. Is a particular school rule or new law a reasonable protection of a "compelling state interest," or is it an "experiment on our liberties"? Who should decide what can be said, typed into a computer, or read—elected lawmakers? the school board? spiritual leaders? community standards? nine Supreme Court Justices in Washington, D.C.? no one? These are difficult questions. For the present, perhaps the words of Justice Abe Fortas can serve as a guide:

> Students in school as well as out of school are persons under our Constitution. They are possessed of fundamental rights which the State must respect, just as they themselves must respect their obligations to the State. . . .[9]

Questions for Discussion

1. A man in New York was convicted for speaking without a permit on the street. He was preaching against certain religions and creating a disturbance. The Supreme Court ruled that the man's conviction violated the First Amendment, but one Justice complained that now "[New York] must place its streets at [the man's] service to hurl insults at the passerby." (*Kunz* v. *New York*) To whom do the streets of New York belong? What limits should be placed on their use? Support your answer.

2. If a city or other agency or group is found to have violated someone's First Amendment rights, what should be done about it? Make some suggestions and then read some of the cases described in the book to find out what happened in specific instances. For example, quite often, the victim's attorney fees are paid by the other side, but the winning side may win very little in terms of money. Why do you think this happens?

3. Some people say we should add more amendments to the Constitution. This could involve opening a new Constitutional Convention, at which the whole original Constitution could be revised. Lawrence Tribe says this could cause a "crisis." William Dudley says "the American public might not be educated enough . . . to vote wisely on a new Constitution." Do you agree?

4. Think about the facts in the situations that follow. Keep in mind what one Chief Justice of the Supreme Court has advised: that wisdom in deciding constitutional questions calls for us to distinguish between "real threat and mere shadow."

- A public school includes a statement in a science text that it is possible that God created the universe. A sticker on the book's title page says that this school district does not necessarily endorse any theories discussed in the book. Is there an establishment of religion?

- An online bulletin board carries a "recipe" for a making a nuclear bomb. Should lawmakers forbid this sort of communication? Would your answer change if the "recipe" was included in a newspaper article? A Prison bulletin board? What if the "recipe" came with instructions to use the bomb on a certain group's headquarters? on the White House?

- A public school sports team is for boys only. A girl demands to be included. What factors might you consider? How many of them arise from the Constitution?

- A public counseling center is supported by taxes, and one counselor wants to wear a pin that says "Jesus loves you," and to encourage his counselees to read the Bible. He insists that this has to be a part of his approach as a counselor. What rights of the counselor and the counselee are involved? Is the counselor violating the Establishment Clause? Would your answer change if the counseling center was in a prison? in a school?

The Constitution of the United States

The text of the Constitution is presented here. All words are given their modern spelling and capitalization. Brackets [ ] indicate parts that have been changed or set aside by amendments.

Preamble

We the people of the United States, in order to form a more perfect Union, establish justice, insure domestic tranquility, provide for the common defense, promote the general welfare, and secure the blessings of liberty to ourselves and our posterity, do ordain and establish this Constitution for the United States of America.

Article I
The Legislative Branch

Section 1. All legislative powers herein granted shall be vested in a Congress of the United States, which shall consist of a Senate and House of Representatives.

The House of Representatives

Section 2. (1) The House of Representatives shall be composed of members chosen every second year by the people of the several states, and the electors in each state shall have the qualifications requisite for electors of the most numerous branch of the state legislature.

(2) No person shall be a representative who shall not have attained the age of twenty-five years, and been seven years a citizen of the United States, and who shall not, when elected, be an inhabitant of that state in which he shall be chosen.

(3) Representatives and direct taxes shall be apportioned among the several states which may be included within this Union, according to their respective numbers, [which shall be determined by adding to the whole number of free persons, including those bound to service for a term of years, and excluding Indians not taxed, three-fifths of all other persons]. The actual enumeration shall be made within three years after the first meeting of the Congress of the United States, and within every subsequent term of ten years, in such manner as they shall by law direct. The number of representatives shall not exceed one for every thirty thousand, but each state shall have at least one representative; [and until such enumeration shall be made, the state of New Hampshire shall be entitled to choose three, Massachusetts eight, Rhode Island and Providence Plantations one, Connecticut five, New York six, New Jersey four, Pennsylvania eight, Delaware one, Maryland six, Virginia ten, North Carolina five, South Carolina five, and Georgia three].

(4) When vacancies happen in the representation from any state, the executive authority thereof shall issue writs of election to fill such vacancies.

(5) The House of Representatives shall choose their Speaker and other officers; and shall have the sole power of impeachment.

The Senate

Section 3. (1) The Senate of the United States shall be composed of two senators from each state, [chosen by the legislature thereof,] for six years; and each senator shall have one vote.

(2) Immediately after they shall be assembled in consequence of the first election, they shall be divided as equally as may be into three classes. The seats of the senators of the first class shall be vacated at the expiration of the second year, of the second class at the expiration of the fourth year, and of the third class at the expiration of the sixth year, so that one-third may be chosen every second year; [and if vacancies happen by resignation, or otherwise, during the recess of the legislature of any state, the executive thereof may make temporary appointments until the next meeting of the legislature, which shall then fill such vacancies].

(3) No person shall be a senator who shall not have attained to the age of thirty years, and been nine years a citizen of the United States, and who shall not, when elected, be an inhabitant of that state for which he shall be chosen.

(4) The Vice President of the United States shall be president of the Senate, but shall have no vote, unless they be equally divided.

(5) The Senate shall choose their other officers, and also a president *pro tempore*, in the absence of the Vice President, or when he shall exercise the office of President of the United States.

(6) The Senate shall have the sole power to try all impeachments. When sitting for that purpose, they shall be on oath or affirmation. When the President of the United States is tried, the Chief Justice shall preside: and no person shall be convicted without the concurrence of two-thirds of the members present.

(7) Judgement in cases of impeachment shall not extend further than to removal from office, and disqualification to hold and enjoy any office of honor, trust, or profit under the United States: but the party convicted shall nevertheless be liable and subject to indictment, trial, judgement and punishment, according to law.

Organization of Congress

Section 4. (1) The times, places and manner of holding elections for senators and representatives, shall be prescribed in each state by the legislature thereof; but the Congress may at any time by law make or alter such regulations, [except as to the places of choosing senators].

(2) The Congress shall assemble at least once in every year, [and such meeting shall be on the first Monday in December], unless they by law appoint a different day.

Section 5. (1) Each house shall be the judge of the elections, returns and qualifications of its own members, and a majority of each shall constitute a quorum to do business; but a smaller number may adjourn from day to day, and may be authorized to compel the attendance of absent members, in such manner, and under such penalties as each house may provide.

(2) Each house may determine the rules of its proceedings, punish its members for disorderly behavior, and, with the concurrence of two-thirds, expel a member.

(3) Each house shall keep a journal of its proceedings, and from time to time publish the same, excepting such parts as may in their judgement require secrecy; and the yeas and nays of the members of either house on any question shall, at the desire of one-fifth of those present, be entered on the journal.

(4) Neither house, during the session of Congress, shall, without the consent of the other, adjourn for more than three days, nor to any other place than that in which the two houses shall be sitting.

Section 6. (1) The senators and representatives shall receive a compensation for their services, to be ascertained by law, and paid out of the treasury of the United States. They shall in all cases, except treason, felony and breach of the peace, be privileged from arrest during their attendance at the session of their respective houses, and in going to and returning from the same; and for any speech or debate in either house, they shall not be questioned in any other place.

(2) No senator or representative shall, during the time for which he was elected, be appointed to any civil office under the authority of the United States, which shall have been created, or the emoluments whereof shall have been increased during such time; and no person holding any office under the United States shall be a member of either house during his continuance in office.

Section 7. (1) All bills for raising revenue shall originate in the House of Representatives; but the Senate may propose or concur with amendments as on other bills.

(2) Every bill which shall have passed the House of Representatives and the Senate, shall, before it become a law, be presented to the President of the United States; if he approve he shall sign it, but if not he shall return it, with his objections to that house in which it shall have originated, who shall enter the objections at large on their journal, and proceed to reconsider it. If after such reconsideration two-thirds of that house shall agree to pass the bill, it shall be sent, together with the objections, to the other house, by which it shall likewise be reconsidered, and if approved by two-thirds of that house, it shall become a law. But in all such cases the votes of both houses shall be determined by yeas and nays, and the names of the persons voting for and against the bill shall be entered on the journal of each house respectively. If any bill shall not be returned by the President within ten days (Sundays excepted) after it shall have been presented to him, the same shall be a law, in like manner as if he had signed it, unless the Congress by their

adjournment prevent its return, in which case it shall not be a law.

(3) Every order, resolution, or vote to which the concurrence of the Senate and House of Representatives may be necessary (except on a question of adjournment) shall be presented to the President of the United States; and before the same shall take effect, shall be approved by him, or being disapproved by him, shall be repassed by two-thirds of the Senate and House of Representatives, according to the rules and limitations prescribed in the case of a bill.

Powers Granted to Congress

The Congress shall have power:

Section 8. (1) To lay and collect taxes, duties, imposts and excises, to pay the debts and provide for the common defense and general welfare of the United States; but all duties, imposts and excises shall be uniform throughout the United States;

(2) To borrow money on the credit of the United States;

(3) To regulate commerce with foreign nations, and among the several states, and with the Indian tribes;

(4) To establish an uniform rule of naturalization, and uniform laws on the subject of bankruptcies throughout the United States;

(5) To coin money, regulate the value thereof, and of foreign coin, and fix the standard of weights and measures;

(6) To provide for the punishment of counterfeiting the securities and current coin of the United States;

(7) To establish post offices and post roads;

(8) To promote the progress of science and useful arts, by securing for limited times to authors and inventors the exclusive right to their respective writings and discoveries;

(9) To constitute tribunals inferior to the Supreme Court;

(10) To define and punish piracies and felonies committed on the high seas, and offenses against the law of nations;

(11) To declare war, grant letters of marque and reprisal, and make rules concerning captures on land and water;

(12) To raise and support armies, but no appropriation of money to that use shall be for a longer term than two years;

(13) To provide and maintain a navy;

(14) To make rules for the government and regulation of the land and naval forces;

(15) To provide for calling forth the militia to execute the laws of the Union, suppress insurrections and repel invasions;

(16) To provide for organizing, arming, and disciplining the militia, and for governing such part of them as may be employed in the service of the United States, reserving to the states respectively, the appointment of the officers, and the authority of training the militia according to the discipline prescribed by Congress;

(17) To exercise exclusive legislation in all cases whatsoever, over such district (not exceeding ten miles square) as may, by cession of particular states, and the acceptance of Congress, become the seat of the government of the United States, and to exercise like authority over all places purchased by the consent of the legislature of the state in which the same shall be, for the erection of forts, magazines, arsenals, dockyards, and other needful buildings;—And

(18) To make all laws which shall be necessary and proper for carrying into execution the foregoing powers, and all other powers vested by this Constitution in the government of the United States, or in any department or officer thereof.

Powers Forbidden to Congress

Section 9. (1) The migration or importation of such persons as any of the states now existing shall think proper to admit, shall not be prohibited by the Congress prior to the year one thousand eight hundred and eight, but a tax or duty may be imposed on such importation, not exceeding ten dollars for each person.

(2) The privilege of the writ of *habeas corpus* shall not be suspended, unless when in cases of rebellion or invasion the public safety may require it.

(3) No bill of attainder or *ex post facto* law shall be passed.

(4) No capitation, [or other direct,] tax shall be laid, unless in proportion to the census or enumeration herein before directed to be taken.

(5) No tax or duty shall be laid on articles exported from any state.

(6) No preference shall be given by any regulation of commerce or revenue to the ports of one state over those of another: nor shall vessels bound to, or from, one state, be obliged to enter, clear, or pay duties in another.

(7) No money shall be drawn from the treasury, but in consequence of appropriations made by law; and a regular statement and account of the receipts and expenditures of all public money shall be published from time to time.

(8) No title of nobility shall be granted by the United States: And no person holding any office or profit or trust under them, shall, without the consent of the Congress, accept of any present, emolument, office, or title, of any kind whatsoever, from any king, prince, or foreign state.

Powers Forbidden to the States

Section 10. (1) No state shall enter into any treaty, alliance, or confederation; grant letters of marque and reprisal; coin money; emit bills of credit; make any thing but gold and silver coin a tender in payment of debts; pass any bill of attainder, *ex post facto* law, or law impairing the obligation of contracts, or grant any title of nobility.

(2) No state shall, without the consent of the Congress, lay any imposts or duties on imports or exports, except what may be absolutely necessary for executing its inspection laws: and the net produce of all duties and imposts, laid by any state on imports or exports, shall be for the use of the treasury of the United States, and all such laws shall be subject to the revision and control of the Congress.

(3) No state shall, without the consent of Congress, lay any duty of tonnage, keep troops, or ships of war in time of peace, enter into any agreement or compact with another state, or with a foreign power, or engage in war, unless actually invaded, or in such imminent danger as will not admit of delay.

Article II
The Executive Branch

Section 1. (1) The executive power shall be vested in a President of the United States of America. He shall hold his office during the term of four years, and, together with the Vice President, chosen for the same term, be elected as follows:

(2) Each state shall appoint, in such manner as the legislature thereof may direct, a number of electors, equal to the whole number of senators and representatives to which the state may be entitled in the Congress: but no senator or representative, or person holding an office of trust or profit under the United States, shall be appointed an elector.

(3) [The electors shall meet in their respective states, and vote by ballot for two persons, of whom one at least shall not be an inhabitant of the same state with themselves. And they shall make a list of all the persons voted for, and of the number of votes for each; which list they shall sign and certify, and transmit sealed to the seat of government of the United States, directed to the president of the Senate. The president of the Senate shall, in the presence of the Senate and House of Representatives, open all the certificates, and the votes shall then be counted. The person having the greatest number of votes shall be the President, if such number be a majority of the whole number of electors appointed; and if there be more than one who have such majority, and have an equal number of votes, then the House of Representatives shall immediately choose by ballot one of them for President; and if no person have a majority, then from the five highest on the list the said House shall in like manner choose the President. But in choosing the President, the votes shall be taken by states, the representation from each state having one vote; a quorum for this purpose shall consist of a member or members from two-thirds of the states, and a majority of all the states shall be necessary to a choice. In every case, after the choice of the President, the person having the greatest number of votes of the electors shall be the Vice President. But if there should remain two or more who have equal votes, the Senate shall choose from them by ballot the Vice President.]

(4) The Congress may determine the time of choosing the electors, and the day on which they shall give their votes; which day shall be the same throughout the United States.

(5) No person except a natural-born citizen, or a citizen of the United States, at the time of the adoption of this Constitution, shall be eligible to the office of President; neither shall any person be eligible to that office who shall not have attained to the age of thirty-five years, and been fourteen years a resident within the United States.

(6) In case of the removal of the President from office, or of his death, resignation, or inability to discharge the powers and duties of the said office, the same shall devolve on the Vice President, and the Congress may by law provide for the case of removal, death, resignation, or inability, both of the President and Vice President, declaring what officer shall then act as President, and such officer shall act accordingly, until the disability be removed, or a President shall be elected.

(7) The President shall, at stated times, receive for his services, a compensation, which shall neither be increased nor diminished during the period for which he shall have been elected, and he shall not receive within that period any other emolument from the United States, or any of them.

(8) Before he enter on the execution of his office, he shall take the following oath or affirmation: "I do solemnly swear (or affirm) that I will faithfully execute the office of the President of the United States, and will to the best of my ability, preserve, protect and defend the Constitution of the United States."

Section 2. **(1)** The President shall be commander-in-chief of the Army and Navy of the United States, and of the militia of the several states, when called into the actual service of the United States; he may require the opinion, in writing, of the principal officer in each of the executive departments, upon any subject relating to the duties of their respective offices, and he shall have power to grant reprieves and pardons for offenses against the United States, except in cases of impeachment.

(2) He shall have power, by and with the advice and consent of the Senate, to make treaties, provided two-thirds of the senators present concur; and he shall nominate, and by and with the advice and consent of the Senate, shall appoint ambassadors, other public ministers and consuls, judges of the Supreme Court, and all other officers of the United States, whose appointments are not herein otherwise provided for, and which shall be established by law: but the Congress may by law vest the appointment of such inferior officers, as they think proper, in the President alone, in the courts of law, or in the heads of departments.

(3) The President shall have the power to fill up all vacancies that may happen during the recess of the Senate, by granting commissions which shall expire at the end of their next session.

Section 3. He shall from time to time give to the Congress information of the state of the Union, and recommend to their consideration such measures as he shall judge necessary and expedient; he may, on extraordinary occasions, convene both houses, or either of them, and in case of disagreement between them, with respect to the time of adjournment, he may adjourn them to such time as he shall think proper; he shall receive ambassadors, and other public ministers; he shall take care that the laws be faithfully executed, and shall commission all the officers of the United States.

Section 4. The President, Vice President and all civil officers of the United States, shall be removed from office on impeachment for, and conviction of, treason, bribery, or other high crimes and misdemeanors.

Article III
The Judicial Branch

Section 1. The judicial power of the United States, shall be vested in one Supreme Court, and in such inferior courts as the Congress may from time to time ordain and establish. The judges, both of the Supreme and inferior courts, shall hold their offices during good behaviour, and shall, at stated times, receive for their services, a compensation, which shall not be diminished during their continuance in office.

Section 2. (1) The judicial power shall extend to all cases, in law and equity, arising under this Constitution, the laws of the United States, and treaties made, or which shall be made, under their authority; —to all cases affecting ambassadors, other public ministers and consuls;—to all cases of admiralty and maritime jurisdiction;—to controversies to which the United States shall be a party;—to controversies between two or more states, [between a state and citizens of another state;], between citizens of different states;—between citizens of the same state claiming lands under grants of different states, and between a state, or the citizens thereof, and foreign states, [citizens or subjects].

(2) In all cases affecting ambassadors, other public ministers and consuls, and those in which a state shall be party, the Supreme Court shall have original jurisdiction. In all the other cases before mentioned, the Supreme Court shall have appellate jurisdiction, both as to law and fact, with such exceptions, and under such regulations as the Congress shall make.

(3) The trial of all crimes, except in cases of impeachment, shall be by jury; and such trial shall be held in the state where the said crimes shall have been committed; but when not committed within any state, the trial shall be at such place or places as the Congress may by law have directed.

Section 3. (1) Treason against the United States shall consist only in levying war against them, or in adhering to their enemies, giving them aid and comfort. No person shall be convicted of treason unless on the testimony of two witnesses to the same overt act, or on confession in open court.

(2) The Congress shall have power to declare the punishment of treason, but no attainder of treason shall work corruption of blood, or forfeiture, except during the life of the person attainted.

Article IV
Relation of the States to Each Other

Section 1. Full faith and credit shall be given in each state to the public acts, records, and judicial proceedings of every other state. And the Congress may by general laws prescribe the manner in which such acts, records and proceedings shall be proved, and the effect thereof.

Section 2. (1) The citizens of each state shall be entitled to all privileges and immunities of citizens in the several states.

(2) A person charged in any state with treason, felony, or other crime, who shall flee justice, and be found in another state, shall on demand of the executive authority of the state from which he fled, be delivered up, to be removed to the state having jurisdiction of the crime.

(3) [No person held to service or labor in one state, under the laws thereof, escaping into another, shall, in consequence of any law or regulation therein, be discharged from such service or labor, but shall be delivered up on claim of the party to whom such service or labor may be due.]

Federal-State Relations

Section 3. (1) New states may be admitted by the Congress into this Union; but no new state shall be formed or erected within the jurisdiction of any other state, nor any state be formed by the junction of two or more states, without the consent of the legislatures of the states concerned as well as of the Congress.

(2) The Congress shall have power to dispose of and make all needful rules and regulations respecting the territory or other property belonging to the United States; and nothing in this Constitution shall be so

construed as to prejudice any claims of the United States, or of any particular state.

Section 4. The United States shall guarantee to every state in this Union, a republican form of government, and shall protect each of them against invasion; and on application of the legislature, or of the executive (when the legislature cannot be convened), against domestic violence.

Article V
Amending the Constitution

The Congress, whenever two-thirds of both houses shall deem it necessary, shall propose amendments to this Constitution, or, on the application of the legislatures of two-thirds of the several states, shall call a convention for proposing amendments, which, in either case, shall be valid to all intents and purposes, as part of this Constitution, when ratified by the legislatures of three-fourths of the several states, or by conventions in three-fourths thereof, as the one or the other mode of ratification may be proposed by the Congress; provided [that no amendment which may be made prior to the year one thousand eight hundred and eight, shall in any manner affect the first and fourth clauses in the ninth section of the first article; and] that no state, without its consent, shall be deprived of its equal suffrage in the Senate.

Article VI
National Debts

(1) All debts contracted and engagements entered into, before the adoption of this Constitution, shall be as valid against the United States under this Constitution, as under the Confederation.

Supremacy of the National Government

(2) This Constitution, and the laws of the United States which shall be made in pursuance thereof; and all treaties made, or which shall be made, under the authority of the United States shall be the supreme law of the land; and the judges in every state shall be bound thereby, any thing in the constitution or laws of any state to the contrary notwithstanding.

(3) The senators and representatives before mentioned, and the members of the several state legislatures, and all executive and judicial officers, both of the United States and of the several states, shall be bound by oath or affirmation, to support this Constitution; but no religious test shall ever be required as a qualification to any office or public trust under the United States.

Article VII

Ratifying the Constitution

The ratification of the conventions of nine states, shall be sufficient for the establishment of this Constitution between the states so ratifying the same.

Done in convention by the unanimous consent of the states present the seventeenth day of September in the year of our Lord one thousand seven hundred and eighty-seven and of the independence of the United States of America the twelfth. In witness whereof we have hereunto subscribed our names.

Amendments to the Constitution

The first ten amendments, known as the Bill of Rights, were proposed on September 25, 1789. They were ratified, or accepted, on December 15, 1791. They were adopted because some states refused to approve the Constitution unless a Bill of Rights, protecting individuals from various unjust acts of government, was added.

Amendment 1

Freedom of religion, speech, and the press; rights of assembly and petition

Amendment 2

Right to bear arms

Amendment 3

Housing of soldiers

Amendment 4

Search and arrest warrants

Amendment 5

Rights in criminal cases

Amendment 6

Rights to a fair trial

Amendment 7

Rights in civil cases

Amendment 8

Bails, fines, and punishments

Amendment 9

Rights retained by the people

Amendment 10

Powers retained by the states and the people

Amendment 11

Lawsuits against states

Amendment 12

Election of the President and Vice President

Amendment 13

Abolition of slavery

Amendment 14

Civil rights

Amendment 15

African-American suffrage

Amendment 16

Income taxes

Amendment 17

Direct election of senators

Amendment 18

Prohibition of liquor

Amendment 19

Women's suffrage

Amendment 20

Terms of the President and Congress

Amendment 21

Repeal of prohibition

Amendment 22

Presidential term limits

Amendment 23

Suffrage in the District of Columbia

Amendment 24

Poll taxes

Amendment 25

Presidential disability and succession

Amendment 26

Suffrage for eighteen-year-olds

Amendment 27

Congressional salaries

Chapter Notes

Chapter 1

1. Clarence B. Carson, *The Rebirth of Liberty* (Irvington-on-Hudson, N.Y.: The Foundation for Economic Education, 1976), p. 218.

2. David Barton, "The Race Card," *The WallBuilder Report* (Aledo, Tex.: Wallbuilders, Inc., Fall 1995), pp. 1–4.

3. M. Stanton Evans, *The Theme is Freedom* (Washington, D.C.: Regnery Publishing, Inc., 1994), pp. 254, 260–261.

4. David Barton, *Keys to Good Government* (Aledo, Tex.: Wallbuilders Press, 1994), p. 19.

5. R.N. Carew Hunt, *The Theory and Practice of Communism* (New York: Penguin, 1964), pp. 113–114.

6. Hezekiah Niles, *Principals and Acts of the Revolution in America* (Baltimore: William Ogden Niles, 1822), p. 418 (quoted in David Barton, *The Spirit of the American Revolution* (Aledo, Tex.: Wallbuilders Press, 1994), p. 10).

7. Michael Oakeshott, ed., *The Social and Political Doctrines of Contemporary Europe* (New York: Cambridge University Press, 1949), p. 227, as quoted in Evans, p. 50.

8. Friedrich Nietzsche, *The Will to Power* (New York: Gordon Press Publishers, 1974), p. 33.

9. Adolf Hitler, *Mein Kampf* (New York: Reynal and Hitchcock, 1939), p. 631.

10. Charles E. Rice, *The Supreme Court and Public Prayer* (New York: Fordham University Press, 1964), p. 160.

11. Hitler, p. 670.

12. Verna G. Hall, ed., *The Christian History of the Constitution* (New York: American Christian Constitution Press, 1962), p. 248.

13. Evans, p. 52.

14. *The Confession of Faith of the Presbyterian Church in America* (Atlanta: General Assembly of the Presbyterian Church in America, 1986), p. xvi.

15. Evans, p. 62.

16. Raoul Berger, *Federalism: The Founders' Design* (Norman, Okla.: University of Oklahoma Press, 1987), p. 27.

17. Evans, p. 53.

18. William D. Graves, "The Bill of Rights, Its Purpose and Meaning and 14th Amendment Incorporation: Original and Current Understandings," *The Journal of Christian Reconstruction*, Vol. XIII, No. 2, 1994, p. 164.

19. Linda Carlson Johnson, *Our Constitution* (Brookfield, Conn.: The Millbrook Press, 1992), p. 34.

20. Carson, p. 217.

21. *Church of Lukumi Babalu Aye* v. *City of Hialeah*, 508 U.S. 521 (1993).

22. Tamara Henry, "Religious Guidance," *USA Today*, August 22, 1995, pp. 1D, 4D.

23. Scott De Nicola, "Beware of V-Chip Talk in 'Family-Values' Speeches," *Citizen*, April 22, 1996, p. 11.

24. Religious Freedom Restoration Act 42 U.S. 2000b (1993), in response to *Employment Division* v. *Smith*, 494 U.S. 872 (1990), and *City of Boerne, Texas* v. *P.F. Flores*, 1997 WL 345322 Sup. Crt., 1997.

Chapter 2

1. Duane Bradley, *The Newspaper: Its Place in a Democracy* (Princeton, N.J.: D. Van Nostrand Co. Inc., 1965), p. 74.

2. J. Edward Evans, *Freedom of Speech* (Minneapolis: Lerner Publication Co., 1990), p. 17.

3. *City of Ladue* v. *Gilleo*, 114 S. Ct. 2038 (1994).

4. *Hague* v. *CIO*, 307 U.S. 496, 515–516 (1939).

5. John Whitehead, *The Right to Picket and the Freedom of Public Discourse* (Westchester, Ill.: Crossway Books, 1984), p. 97.

6. Ibid., pp. 108–110.

7. John E. Nowak, Ronald D. Rotunda, and J. Nelson, *Constitutional Law,* 3rd ed. (St. Paul, Minn.: West Publishing Co., 1986), Sec. 16.9, p. 846.

8. *Forsyth County* v. *Nationalist Movement*, 505 U.S. 123 (1992).

9. *United States* v. *Grace*, 461 U.S. 171 (1983).

10. Nowak et al., ibid., Sec. 16.5, p. 834.

11. Ibid.

12. *Schenck* v. *United States*, 249 U.S. 47, 52 (1919).

13. Elder Witt, *Guide to the U.S. Supreme Court*, 2d ed. (Washington, D.C.: Congressional Quarterly, 1990), p. 395.

14. Ibid.

15. *Chaplinsky* v. *New Hampshire*, 315 U.S. 568, 572 (1942).

16. *Brandenburg* v. *Ohio*, 395 U.S. 444, 446 (1969).

17. Final Report of the Attorney General's Commission on Pornography, (Nashville: Rutledge Press, 1986), pp. 11–13.

18. *Commonwealth* v. *Friede*, 171 N.E. 472 (1930).

19. *Roth* v. *United States* 354 U.S. 476, 485 (1957).

20. Ibid., at 487.

21. *Federal Communications Commission* v. *Pacifica Foundation*, 438 U.S. 726 (1978).

22. *Carlin Communications, Inc.* v. *Southern Bell Telegraph and Telephone Company,* 802 F. 2d 1352 (11th Cir., 1986); "TV Station Manager Puts Families Before Friends," *Citizen*, April 22, 1996, p. 14.

23. Nowak, ibid., Sec. 16.18, p. 882, citing *FCC* v. *League of Women Voters.*

24. *Miami Herald* v. *Tornillo*, 418 U.S. 241 (1974).

25. Witt, p. 417.

26. *Board of Trustees of the State University of New York* v. *Fox*, 492 U.S. 469 (1989).

27. *Capital Broadcasting Co.* v. *Acting Attorney General Kleindienst*, 405 U.S. 1000 (1972), affirming without opinion 333 F. Supp. 582 (D.D.C. 1971).

28. *Posadas de Puerto Rico Associates* v. *Tourism Council of Puerto Rico*, 478 U.S. 328, 1986.

29. Zechariah Chafee, *Free Speech in the United States* (New York: Atheneum, 1969), pp. 405–406.

30. *Breard* v. *City of Alexandria*, 341 U.S. 622, 642 (1951); *Martin* v. *City of Struthers*, 319 U.S. 141, 145–146 (1943).

31. *Ward* v. *Rock Against Racism*, 491 U.S. 781, 796 (1989).

32. Mary Abbe, "Bloody performance draws criticism," *Minneapolis Star-Tribune*, March 24, 1994, p. 1A.

33. *Terminiello* v. *Chicago*, 337 U.S. 1(1949).

34. *Tinker* v. *Des Moines Independent Community School District*, 393 U.S. 503, 506 (1969).

35. *Butts* v. *Dallas Independent School District*, 436 F. 2d 728, 732 (5th Cir. 1971).

36. Stephen R. Goldstein and E. Gordon Gee, *Law and Public Education* (New York: The Michie Co. and The Bobbs-Merrill Co., Inc., Publishers 1980), p. 230.

37. *United States* v. *O'Brien*, 391 U.S. 367 (1968); *Bethel School District* v. *Fraser*, 478 U.S. 675 (1986).

38. *Texas* v. *Johnson*, 491 U.S. 397, 1989.

39. *Hurley et al.* v. *Irish-American Gay, Lesbian, and Bisexual Group of Boston*, 115 S. Ct. 2338 (1995)

40. *Wooley* v. *Maynard*, 430 U.S. 705 (1977).

41. *The Intellectual Freedom Manual*, 4th ed. (Chicago: American Library Association, 1992), p. 71.

42. John Douglas and Mark Olshaker, "Effective Crime Fighting Requires Informed Public," *USA Today*, August 18, 1997, p. 13A.

43. Ibid.

44. *Rust* v. *Sullivan*, 500 U.S. 173 (1991).

45. Thomas I. Emerson, "Free Speech," *Encyclopedia of the American Constitution,* Leonard W. Levy, ed., (New York: MacMillan, 1986), p. 795.

46. 20 U.S.C.A. 1232

47. Whitehead, p. 61.

48. Bradley, p. 75.

Chapter 3

1. J. Edward Evans, *Freedom of the Press* (Minneapolis: Lerner Publishing Co., 1990), p. 25.

2. Duane Bradley, *The Newspaper: Its Place in a Democracy* (Princeton, N.J.: D. Van Nostrand Co., Inc., 1965), p. 3.

3. Evans, p. 8.

4. Bradley, p. 4.

5. Ibid., p. 65.

6. Michael Schudson, *Discovering the News* (New York: Basic Books, Inc., 1978), p. 16.

7. James Fenimore Cooper, *The American Democrat* (Baltimore: Penguin Books, 1969), p. 183.

8. John E. Nowak, Ronald D. Rotunda. and J. Nelson Young, *Constitutional Law*, 3rd ed. (St. Paul, Minn.: West Publishing Co., 1986), Sec. 16.4, pp. 832–833.

9. Evans, p. 41.

10. Robert Spiller, Willard Thorp, et al., eds., *Literary History of the United States,* 4th ed. (New York: Macmillan Publishing Co., Inc., 1975), p. 1134.

11. Ibid.

12. Evans, p. 43.

13. Ibid., p. 45.

14. *New York Times Co.* v. *United States*, 403 U.S. 713, 723–724.

15. *Black's Law Dictionary*, 6th ed., West Publishing Co., 1991, p. 67.

16. Ibid.

17. *New York Times* v. *Sullivan*, 376 U.S. 254 (1964).

18. *Hustler Magazine* v. *Falwell*, 485 U.S. 46 (1988).

19. 335 U.S. 848 (1948).

20. Lon Tweeten's illustration for "On-line Goldmine," *USA Today*, February 18, 1996, quoting sources at Morgan Stanley, p. 4F.

21. Scott DeNicola, "Beware of V-Chip Talk in 'Family-Values Speeches," *Citizen*, April 22, 1996, p. 11.

22. *Hazelwood Independent School District* v. *Kuhlmeier*, 484 U.S. 260 (1988).

23. Robert Reynolds, "Hazelwood's Landmark Principal Tells his Behind-the-Scenes Story," *The Executive Educator*, September 1988, pp. 16–17.

24. Ibid.

25. Ibid., p. 30.

26. *Rosenberger et al.* v. *Rector and Visitors of the University of Virginia*, Slip opinion, No. 94–329, June 29, 1995, p. 3.

27. Ibid., p. 4.

28. *Rosenberger,* p. 15.

29. Nowak, Sec. 16.19, p. 886.

30. *Pell* v. *Procunier,* 417 U.S. 817, 834 (1974).

31. Nowak, Sec. 16.21, p. 889; Sec. 16.25, p. 896; *Nixon* v. *Warner Communications, Inc.*, 435 U.S. 589, 1978.

32. "Viewpoint: The Media and the Trial," ABC Telecast, October 6, 1995. Cases involving *Chandler* v. *Florida*, 449 U.S. 560 (1981) and *Waller* v. *Georgia*, 467 U.S. 39 (1984).

33. Owen Fiss, "Free Speech and Social Structure," 71 *Iowa Law Review* (1986), pp. 1405, 1408, 1410.

34. Interview with Bob Losure, CNN News, Tulsa, Okla., January 30, 1996.

Chapter 4

1. Thomas Jefferson, *Jefferson Writings,* ed. Merrill D. Peterson (New York: Literary Classics of the United States, Inc., 1984), p. 1475.

2. Perry Miller and Thomas Johnson, eds., *The Puritans* (New York: Harper, 1963), p. 227; Robert L. Cord, *Separation of Church and State* (New York: Lambeth Press, 1982), pp. 179, 192–193 .

3. Jonathan Elliott, *Debates on the Federal Constitution* (Philadelphia: J.B. Lippincott Co., 1901), Vol. II, p. 553.

4. Justice Joseph Story, *Commentaries on the Constitution*, Sec. 1879 pp. 596–597.

5. *Everson* v. *Board of Education*, 330 U.S. 1 (1947).

6. Annals, p. 328.

7. *Gales and Seaton's History of Debates in Congress*, August 15, 1789, cited in M. Stanton Evans, *The Theme is Freedom: Religion, Politics, and the American Tradition* (Washington, D.C.: Regnery Publishing, Inc., 1994), p. 282.

8. Quoted in David Barton, *The Myth of Separation* (Aledo, Tex.: Wall Builder Press, 1992), p. 125.

9. Ibid., p. 118.

10. Quoted in Jared Sparks, *The Life of Governeur Morris* (Boston: Gray and Bowen, 1832), Vol. III, p. 483.

11. William J. Federer, *America's God and Country: Encyclopedia of Quotations* (Coppell, Tex.: 1994), p. 660.

12. John Witherspoon, *The Works of the Reverend John Witherspoon* (Philadelphia: William W. Woodard, 1802), Vol. III, p. 46.

13. Ibid., p. 47.

14. William D. Graves, "Did the Framers Mandate a Wall of Separation between Church and State? The Original Understanding," *The Oklahoma Bar Journal*, Vol. 58, no. 39, October 31, 1987, p. 2988.

15. Ibid.

16. Herbert Lockyer, *The Last Words of Saints and Sinners* (Grand Rapids, Mich.: Kregel, 1969), p. 98.

17. *Church of the Holy Trinity* v. *United States* 143 U.S. 457 (1892).

18. John Eidsmoe, *Christianity and the Constitution* (Grand Rapids, Mich.: Baker Book House, 1987), p. 243.

19. Paul L. Ford, *Life of Jefferson* (Cambridge, Mass.: A.W. Elson and Co., 1904), Vol. IX, p. 174.

20. Jethro Lieberman, "Freedom of Conscience: Separating Church and State,"*Oklahoma Bar Journal*, Vol. 58, no. 39, October 31, 1987, p. 2994.

21. *Illinois ex rel. McCollum* v. *Board of Education*, 333 U.S. 203 (1948); *Zorach* v. *Clauson*, 343 U.S. 306 (1952); *Lanner* v. *Wimmer*, 662 F. 2d 1349 (10th Cir. 1981).

22. 403 U.S. 602, 614 (1971).

23. 465 U.S. 668, 1985.

24. *Capitol Square Review and Advisory Board* v. *Pinette*, 63 Law Week 4684, June 29, 1995, at 64 LW 1002.

25. *Lamb's Chapel* v. *Center Moriches*, 113 S. Ct., 2147 (1993).

26. Author interview with Rita Woltz, legal coordinator, Rutherford Institute, Charlottesville, VA, August 18, 1997.

27. Letter from President Bill Clinton to Congressman Henry Hyde, quoted on "Jay Sekulow Live," Virginia Beach, Va.: "American Center for Law and Justice" radio program March 14, 1996.

28. James Madison, Memorial and Remonstrance against Religious Assessments, 1785, in Cord, p. 245.

29. John Bartlett, *Bartlett's Familiar Quotations* (Boston: Little, Brown and Company, 1980), p. 383.

Chapter 5

1. *Zorach* v. *Clauson*, 72 S. Ct. 679, 684, 1952.

2. Civil Rights Act of 1964, 42 U.S.C. 2000e (j).

3. *Zorach* v. *Clauson*, 72 S. Ct. 679, 684, 1952; *Lanner* v. *Wimmer*, 662 F. 2d 349, 10th Cir. 1981.

4. *Board of Airport Commissioners* v. *Jews for Jesus, Inc.*, 482 U.S. 569 (1987).

5. *Heffron* v. *International Society for Krishna Consciousness*, 452 U.S. 640 (1981).

6. Thomas Jefferson, January 1, 1802, letter to the Danbury Baptist Association, quoted in *Reynolds* v. *United States*, 98 U.S. 164 (1878).

7. *Lamont* v. *Postmaster General*, 381 U.S. 301, 308 (1965), Justice Brennan concurring .

8. *Cantwell* v. *Connecticut*, 310 U.S. 269 (1940).

9. Ibid., at 304.

10. See, for example, *Phoenix Elementary School District No. 1* v. *Green*, 1997 WL 149726 (Ariz. App. Div. 2), March 27, 1997.

11. Tamara Henry, "Religious Guidance: Clinton Directive Tries to Clarify Activities Allowed," *USA Today*, August 22, 1995, p. 4D.

12. W.W. Sweet, *Religion in the Development of American Culture* (New York: Peter Smith, 1963), p. 50.

13. *Westside Community Schools* v. *Mergens*, 496 U.S. 226 (1990).

14. *Wisconsin* v. *Yoder*, 406 U.S. 205, 1972.

15. 268 U.S. 510 (1925).

16. John Naisbitt, *Megatrends* (New York: Warner Books, 1982), p. 144.

Chapter 6

1. *NAACP* v. *Alabama ex. rel. Patterson*, 357 U.S. 449, 460–461 (1964).

2. Laurence H. Tribe, *Constitutional Law*, 2nd ed. (Mineola, N.Y.: The Foundation Press, Inc., 1988), p. 1297.

3. Ibid., p. 1300.

4. *Restatement of the Law, Trusts*, 2nd ed. (St Paul, Minn.: American Law Institute Publishers, 1987), Chapter 2, Section 62.

5. *Bowers* v. *Hardwick*, 478 U.S. 186 (1986).

6. *Police Department of Chicago* v. *Mosley*, 408 U.S. 92; *Grayned* v. *City of Rockford*, 408 U.S. 104.

7. *NAACP* v. *Alabama ex rel. Patterson*, 377 U.S. 288 (1964).

8. John E. Nowak, Ronald D. Rotunda, and J. Nelson Young, *Constitutional Law*, 3rd ed. (St. Paul, Minn.: West Publishing Co., 1986), pp. 956–957.

9. *Abood* v. *Detroit Board of Education*, 431 U.S. 209 (1977).

10. Elder Witt, *Guide to the U.S. Supreme Court*, 2nd ed. (Washington, D.C.: Congressional Quarterly, Inc., 1990), p. 30.

11. *Congressional Roll Call* (Washington, D.C.: Congressional Quarterly, Inc., 1994), p. 62.

12. John Whitehead, *The Right to Picket and the Freedom of Public Discourse* (Westchester, N.Y.: Greenway Books, 1984), p. 28.

13. Ibid.

Chapter 7

1. *Schenck* v. *Pro Choice of Western New York*, 96 U.S. 1065 (1996).

2. *Board of County Commissioners* v. *Umbehr* 116 U.S. 2342 (1996).

3. *R.A.V.* v. *St. Paul*, 112 S. Ct. 2538 (1992)

4. Ibid., p. 306.

5. Linzer, "White Liberal Looks at Racist Speech," 65 *St. John's Law Review*, 187 (1991).

6. Del Jones, "Workplaces May Feel New Push for Religion," *USA Today*, August 18, 1997, p. 1B.

7. Author interview with Rita Woltz, legal coordinator, Rutherford Institute, Charlottesville, VA, August 18, 1997.

8. Ibid.

9. *Tinker* v. *Des Moines*, 393 U.S. 511 (1969).

Glossary

abridge—To limit.

amendment—A change. A constitutional amendment can be proposed either by a vote of two thirds of both houses of Congress, or by holding a national constitutional convention. Three fourths of the states are needed to "ratify" or pass the amendment.

bias—Prejudice or unreasoning preference for or against a group.

boycott—To refrain from purchasing a product or service in order to protest against the seller's beliefs or practices.

censorship—Supression of speech or published material that is considered objectionable.

commercial speech—Communication that attempts to sell something.

contention—A legal position or argument.

defamation—A false statement spread to others that harms a person's reputation. If the defamed person is already well known, defamation occurs only when the speaker intended to hurt his or her victim with lies.

federal—Pertaining to the nation as opposed to a state or local area.

forum—A place and time for free exchange of ideas.

libel—The publication of blasphemous, treasonable, seditious, or obscene writings or pictures.

petition—To make a request.

redress—Compensation for wrong or loss.

sectarian—Pertaining to religion (sometimes referring to certain sects or religious groups).

secular—Nonreligious.

sedition—Rebellion against the government.

Further Reading

For Younger Students

Barton, David. *The Bulletproof George Washington*. Aledo, Tex.: Wallbuilders, Inc., 1990.

D'Aulaire, Ingri, and Edgar Parin. *Benjamin Franklin*. New York: Doubleday, 1957.

——. *George Washington*. New York: Doubleday, 1936.

Evans, J. Edward. *Freedom of the Press*. Minneapolis: Lerner Publications, 1990.

Findlay, Bruce and Esther. *Your Rugged Constitution*. Stanford, Calif.: Stanford University Press, 1987.

Fritz, Jean. *Shh! We're Writing the Constitution*. New York: G.P. Putnam's Sons, 1987.

Johnson, Linda Carlson. *Our Constitution*. Brookfield, Conn.: Millbrook Press, 1992.

For Older Students

Barton, David. *Foundations of American Government* (video or audio). Aledo, Tex.: Wallbuilders, Inc. 1991.

Bradford, M.E. *A Worthy Company*. Marlborough, N.H.: The Plymouth Rock Foundation, 1982.

Bradley, Duane. *The Newspaper: Its Place in a Democracy*. Princeton, N.J.: D. Van Nostrand Co., Inc., 1965.

Eastland, Terry, ed. *Religious Liberty in the Supreme Court*. Washington, D.C.: Ethics and Public Policy Center, 1993.

Haynes, Charles C., and Oliver Thomas, eds. *Finding Common Ground: A First Amendment Guide to Religion and Public Education*. Nashville: The Freedom Forum First Amendment Center, 1994.

Hentoff, Nat. *Free Speech for Me But Not for Thee: How the American Left and Right Relentlessly Censor Each Other*. New York: HarperCollins Publishers, Inc., 1992.

Judson, Karen. *The Constitution of the United States*. Springfield, N.J.: Enslow Publishers, Inc., 1995.

Lieberman, Jethro K. *Free Speech and the Law*. New York: Lothrop, Lee, and Shepard Books, 1980.

Lindop, Edmund. *The Bill of Rights and Landmark Cases*. New York: Franklin Watts, 1989.

Miller, J. Anthony. *Texas* v. *Johnson: The Flag-Burning Case*. Springfield, N.J.: Enslow Publishers, Inc., 1997.

Stein, R. Conrad. *The Bill of Rights*. Chicago: Children's Press, Inc., 1992.

Witt, Elder. *Guide to the United States Supreme Court*, 2d ed. Washington, D.C.: Congressional Quarterly, 1990.

Zeinert, Karen. *Free Speech: From Newspapers to Music Lyrics*. Springfield, N.J.: Enslow Publishers, 1995.

Index